COMMUNITY CARE IN PRACTICE

COMMUNITY CARE IN PRACTICE

edited by
RALPH DAVIDSON AND SUSAN HUNTER

B.T. Batsford · *London*
in association with
British Agencies for Adoption and Fostering

First published 1994
© Ralph Davidson and Susan Hunter 1994

Typeset by J&L Composition Ltd, Filey, North Yorkshire
and printed in Great Britain by Redwood Books, Trowbridge, Wilts

Published by
B.T. Batsford Ltd
4 Fitzhardinge Street
London W1H 0AH

A catalogue record for this book is available from the British Library

ISBN 0 7134 7076 3

Contents

The Contributors

Joan Beck is Chief Inspector of Social Services, Doncaster Metropolitan Council. She is a past President of the Social Care Association and currently Chair of its Social Care Practice Committee.

Bob Bessell is Managing Director of Retirement Security Ltd, which builds and manages private Very Sheltered Housing throughout England. Previously he was a Director of Social Services (Warwickshire, Reading) and a Lecturer in Social Work, University of Keele.

Rosemary Bland is a Lecturer in Social Work at Stirling University and has undertaken several Scottish Office-funded research studies into residential and multidisciplinary care management.

Ralph Davidson is a Senior Lecturer in Social Work at the University of Edinburgh. He formerly worked in the local authority social services as a Senior Child Care Officer, Area Officer and Practice Teacher. He has a particular interest in the organizational contexts of social work practice.

Ashley Dowlen is a Senior Manager with East Sussex County Council Social Services Department.

Norman Flynn is a Research Fellow at the London School of Economics and Political Science. He has worked with Ashley Dowlen on decentralizing the management of social service departments.

David Hunter is Professor of Health Policy and Management, Director of the Nuffield Institute for Health Services Studies and Deputy

Director of Public Health at the University of Leeds. He has worked in various capacities in England and Scotland, publishing widely on aspects of health and social care policy and management.

Susan Hunter is a Lecturer in Social Work at Edinburgh University where she has been involved in developing teaching and research into aspects of services for older people and people with learning disabilities.

Laurie Naumann was Director of the Scottish Council for Single Homeless and Secretary of the Care in the Community Scottish Working Group at the time of writing; currently he is on secondment to the Scottish Office Social Work Services Inspectorate.

Charles Ogden is Chief Social Services Officer, Bromley. He trained originally as a psychiatric social worker and has worked for a variety of local authorities – Rotherham, Northamptonshire, Suffolk, Kent and three London boroughs.

Averil Osborn was Senior Assistant Director of Age Concern Scotland and Honorary Research Fellow of the Nuffield Institute (Leeds University) at the time of writing; she has since joined the Joseph Rowntree Foundation. Her background is in social and health services research.

Naina Patel is Head of the 'Race' Programme at CCETSW. Among other initiatives, she has been responsible for designing and managing a major curriculum project in anti-racist social work education. This has involved over 400 people and has resulted in seven publications.

Jill Pitkeathley is Director of the Carers' National Association and was an advisor to the Griffiths Review of Community Care. In the past she has worked as a social worker and Voluntary Services Co-ordinator as well as holding positions with the National Consumer Council, the CAB (Reading) and Community Council (Berkshire).

Judy Renshaw is a Project Manager at the Audit Commission, currently working on a review of mental health services in England and Wales. Prior to this she was Director of Good Practices in Mental Health.

Pete Ritchie is a self-employed training consultant based in Edinburgh. He has a background in community social work and worked for several years on the All-Wales Strategy for People with Learning Difficulties.

Ian Sinclair has had a varied career in social work and social research. He was previously Director of Research at the National Institute of Social Work and is currently Professor of Social Work at the University of York.

Bill Whyte is a Senior Lecturer in Social Work at the University of Edinburgh. He formerly worked in local authority social services as a Manager and Mental Health Officer. His research interests include guardianship, the role of the mental health officer and young people in trouble.

Anne Yanetta is a Lecturer at the School of Planning and Housing, Heriot-Watt University, Course Director of the Postgraduate Diploma in Housing, and Convener of the Scottish Council for Single Homeless Executive Committee.

Introduction

Adapting to change is not a new experience for local authority social services/work departments. However, the extent of the changes they have been required to accommodate in the early 1990s is massive. The Children Act 1989, which came into force in England in October 1991, introduced major and wide-ranging alterations to the way in which social work services for children, young people and their families are envisaged, delivered, monitored and evaluated. In the same period, changes in criminal justice legislation and the introduction of the national standards for probation and social work in the criminal justice system have required substantial adaptations to the provision of social work services to offenders. Although the new pattern of community care changes has been phased in, starting in April 1991, this has not lessened the impact of what is a fundamental shift in the delivery of and accountability for social work services to adults in need of care and in the relationships between the different statutory, voluntary and independent agencies that have provided these services in recent years.

The tasks involved in organising and preparing to cope with change on this scale have been daunting for both managers and practitioners in the agencies affected. Faced with such substantial change it was easy for them to feel that many of their existing practices and skills were redundant and that the business of devising new management structures and practices and of acquiring new practice skills was overwhelming. Added to this they had to cope with real lack of clarity about whether the Government would provide sufficient funds to sustain the new patterns of service that were being planned and consequently whether these services could be ready for implementation at the required time.

Despite all these difficulties the work of planning and managing these changes in service provision has proceeded and many of the central ideas and principles underlying the new legislation have been widely welcomed. One of these is the commitment in both the Children Act and the community care legislation to giving a stronger voice to the service users – young people, their parents, people who are elderly or disabled and their carers – in the decision making about what they need and about what kinds of services will meet these needs most appropriately. Similarly the emphasis placed on developing quality in service provision and ensuring effective patterns of quality control that will involve consumers has led to the creation of new and better quality control mechanisms in services for children and adults in need of care.

This book attempts to address in straightforward, practical ways many of the new structures, tasks and skills that will be required if the practice of community care is to realise its potential. We chose to pursue a broad approach in the book, covering as many topics as possible and restricting the length of chapter available to each author. We also invited the authors to write, where appropriate, in a way that would enable readers to find in the planning and implementation of community care a continuity of philosophy, policy and practice skill, where these exist, and a clarity about those situations in which they do not and in which entirely new developments were therefore essential.

The book has two parts. In the first we focus on the prospect of community care, considering some of the fundamental philosophical issues involved and the expectations of service providers and consumers. In the second part the emphasis is on the implementation of community care with sections on planning the care, managing the care, packaging the care and monitoring the care. These discuss the implications of implementation for relationships between the statutory social work services and providers of health care, housing, voluntary social services and the independent sector. They also explore some of the new roles involved for local authority social services/work departments as they move from being principally providers of care services to being procurers and contractors of services. These include processes of interdisciplinary assessment, needs led service provision in a context of limited resources and methods of quality assurance and service inspection.

Clearly, there are gaps in the book. For example, we chose not to devote a chapter to gender in relation to community care, which has been covered elsewhere. In a book of this length, however, some gaps are inevitable. Indeed it is open to criticism for having tried to cover too wide a range of topics rather than focus in detail on a few key areas. However, our intention was that the book should provide an introduction to many of the complex issues social work managers and practitioners are having to contend with in planning and implementing community care, rather than be a definitive statement on these. We hope that it will be a useful guide and stimulus to all those involved in this new and challenging development in social policy and social service provision.

SECTION ONE:
THE PROSPECT OF COMMUNITY CARE

1 *Community care – a quick look at some of the big issues* Pete Ritchie

The White Paper *Caring for People* (DOH, 1989) recommends five specific mechanisms for improving the quality and effectiveness of community care: community care planning; the separation of purchaser and provider; assessment and care management; inspection units, and complaints procedures. There are also two significant financial changes: the proposed transfer to local authorities in 1993 of DSS funds for residential care for new clients, and the introduction of the new mental health specific grant; reference will be made to these specific mechanisms later.

This chapter traces some of the immediate causes of the current community care changes, describes some different interpretations of the problem these changes are intended to solve, and suggests what we might see if community care gets better.

Change within pattern, or change of pattern

Caring for People came out about the same time as the Berlin Wall came down. The British Government's commitment in principle to community care goes back at least to the 1959 Mental Health Act – before the Berlin Wall went up. If the pace of change from 1959–89 was slower than a Trabant, the pace of change since has been hardly Porsche-like – particularly for those on the receiving end of community care. But the sense of confusion among practitioners and managers of community care does suggest parallels with perestroika in Eastern Europe and the Soviet Union.

Will anything really change? Will the old power structures simply

7

reassert themselves under new names? What difference will it make to people's everyday quality of life? This chapter goes along with Zhou-en-Lai, who, when asked his opinion of the French Revolution replied 'it's too soon to say' (*Guardian* 2 May 1989). The past history of community care is too full of anomalies to suggest that there is anything inevitable about its future. We are still too close to the threads now being woven into the community care tapestry to see the emerging pattern.

Picking out the threads

Just as the threads of the disintegration in the Soviet Union can be traced back hundreds of years to the expansionist policies of Peter the Great, so the central theme of community care can be traced back to the development of institutional models of care (Wolfensberger, 1975) at the time of the Industrial Revolution. Is segregation – well-intentioned or otherwise – the best or only option for those who need help to survive in this society but have neither friends, family nor money to provide that help? Or is it possible to make society more survivable, more tolerant and more inclusive?

The immediate factors that over the course of the 1980s shaped the current community care changes will be familiar to most readers: the unexpectedly rapid increase in the public subsidy to private residential care, particularly for older people; the continuing imbalance in the resources devoted to community-based services relative to those devoted to residential and hospital care; the evident failure of joint planning (Wistow, 1990, Chapter 8) to deliver strategic co-operation; obvious inefficiencies in the system, considerable dissatisfaction with the quality of statutory community care services, and the Government's ideological commitment to reducing local authorities' size and power.

A whole set of wider trends have also helped to shape the changes. Five of these are briefly described below – others could doubtless to added to the list.

Firstly, the White Paper (1990) is explicitly based on certain values, which may be orthodox now but were not widely held 15 or 20 years ago. The changes outlined in this White Paper are intended to:

● enable people to live as normal a life as possible in their own homes or in a homely environment in the local community

- provide the right amount of care and support to help people achieve maximum possible independence and, by acquiring or reacquiring basic living skills, help them achieve their full potential
- give people a greater individual say in how they lead their lives and the services they need to help them to do so.

Many people would argue that the Government could do much more to put these values into practice but the values themselves do imply the need for significant change in the content as well as the packaging of services.

Secondly, the voluntary and 'not-for-profit' sector – and housing associations in particular – has become more professional and assertive. Traditional voluntary sector provision had always been significant in volume terms but lacking in political influence; the 'new look' voluntary organizations in the 1980s became more up-to-date, better managed, better marketed and more innovative than many statutory organizations.

Thirdly, the purchaser-provider split has been taking root 'across the board' – in health, housing, education, even the civil service. This reflected two parallel trends: the greater emphasis in industry on control through contract rather than ownership and the greater emphasis in policy-making on outcomes rather than process. For example, Nissan assembles cars with components made by dozens of sub-contractors rather than making them in-house; Safeway can get the peas it wants when it wants them without owning the farms.

In policy-making, the splitting of the civil service into semi-autonomous agencies has been accompanied by much tighter expectations of the function and performance of each agency; the move towards local management of schools has been accompanied by the national curriculum and league tables of exam results; hospitals acquiring trust status will only get District Health Authority money for work that reflects regional health priorities as determined by statistics on comparative deaths and illness.

What Fergus Murray (1983) calls 'the decentralisation of production and the centralisation of command' has become a central theme in the way community care is organized. For the first time, local authorities are expected to take an overall responsibility for planning and organizing community care, while providing fewer services directly.

Fourthly, institutional care, despite its apologists, has continued to get a bad press. It was the scandal at Ely Hospital in 1969 that launched

9

the White Paper *Better Services for the Mentally Handicapped*; throughout the last few years there have been reports of abuse of older people in residential care, disabled children in special education, and people treated in psychiatric hospitals.

Finally, users of services have started to become organized and vocal. Two strands of 'user power' have to be distinguished. Much Government guidance advocates choice for users as consumers or customers. In reality, while some users have been able through the Independent Living Fund to exercise private choice using public money, the great majority of users are unable to choose the services they want – either because that power lies elsewhere, or because there is only one service available, or because the sort of service they want is not available at all.

The other strand of user power is genuine involvement in decision making, at an individual and collective level – from choosing your own home help to lobbying for a better regional policy on adapted transport. It is this sort of power that has the potential for transforming the nature of care in the community.

So what is the problem?

The White Paper *Caring for People*, the subsequent NHS and Community Care Act (1990) and a whole edifice of subsequent guidance are clearly intended to promote change. Research institutes spring up; new books are written, and old ones dusted down and reprinted; courses and training packs proliferate. There is no doubt that genuine energy and commitment is being invested by people at all different levels of 'the system'. But what is the problem that these diverse efforts are intended to solve?

The 'balance of care'

On the most narrow interpretation, the problem is that too many older people have to go into or stay in hospital, or in residential or nursing homes, when they want to stay in their own home and could do so at less cost to the public purse. It is this tendency, fuelled by the 'perverse incentive' (Audit Commission, 1986) that has generated the sense of urgency in central government.

The 'solution', unfortunately, is often seen as tighter gatekeeping of residential care rather than the creation of responsive and flexible home care services. More and better assessments, with professionals as arbiters of need, prescribers of solutions and rationers of resources could serve to increase the status of professionals while proving an expensive distraction for service users.

The lack of overall strategy

A broader interpretation of 'the problem' is that the overall system for planning and providing services is disorganized. As Griffiths (HMSO, 1988) noted, 'it is a matter of chance whether a person needing long stay care finds himself in a geriatric ward, or in a nursing home or residential home, with different costs and charging'. To this, he could have added, 'or in sheltered housing, or in his own home', and the same applies to people with mental health problems, learning difficulties and physical disabilities (Fiedler, 1988).

The lack of a coherent overview, and the reluctance of the major agencies to pool resources, means that it is no one's job to understand, let alone sort out, the mess. The solution proposed by the NHS and Community Care Act is community care planning. Time will tell whether those entrusted with the task will have the time, the skills and the freedom to move beyond incremental planning – 'a bit more of the same' – towards a genuine reappraisal of the best way to get the right sort of support to the people who need it most.

There are formidable barriers: professional defensiveness and language barriers; sheer lack of information; the need to think simultaneously about housing, health, social work and social security and across all 'client groups'; and the need to think through tough political and moral issues. What should be the role of the local state? Should people pay for community care if they can afford to? Should we really spend a great deal of money to improve the quality of life of a few people who are very severely disabled, or should we spread that money around?

The first round of community care planning is likely to be very much 'business as usual'; the next two or three rounds will show how far planners are getting their heads round the 'big picture' (Ennis, 1991).

Obsolete models of service provision

A third version of 'the problem' is that the old models of service are bankrupt. Therefore new ways have to be found to hasten the transition

11

to new models: out with people living in hostels and hospitals, in with intensive home care and supported accommodation; out with adult training centres, in with community-based day services and supported employment; out with acute psychiatric admissions, in with crisis intervention teams.

Proponents point to the failure of adult training centres to train, the disabling consequences of residential care, the counter-therapeutic consequences of admission to psychiatric care, the inaccessibility and inappropriateness of 'white' services in a multicultural and multiracial society, and the general lack of clear purpose in many of the 'old-style' services (Beeforth, 1990).

The shift of resources from traditional models to new ones has certainly been slow. Innovative projects often operate alongside traditional services that are based on an opposing philosophy, and that continue to attract the major share of resources, while skilfully resisting change.

Many factors combine to reduce the speed of change: incremental budgeting, overall financial constraints, the psychological dependency on buildings, even those well past their sell-by date; and sometimes just a lack of vision or gumption.

The solution proposed by 'New Right' commentators such as Pirie and Butler (1989) is to give users power to choose directly the service they want to use and to encourage a 'free market' between competing providers. There are a number of arguments against this approach, some about principle, some about practice (Hoggett, 1990).

Firstly, the market may settle down into a situation where a small number of providers offer the same service in different packaging – and for users who do not want baked beans there is no alternative. New services with high start-up costs will find it hard to enter 'the market' in competition with established services with low marginal costs. The pressure from the public purse makes this situation more likely.

Secondly, particularly in rural areas, there may be a single supplier and a single service.

Thirdly, users may make poor choices because they have poor information.

Fourthly, disaggregated individual user choices will not generate collective strategies such as integrated public transport.

Finally, many users do not have the personal power to make choices, negotiate changes, complain, or withdraw their custom, and would need advocates or representatives to help them exercise their authority.

Many people have 'chosen' to go into private or voluntary residential care and thereby to commit public funds, but few of these are seen or see themselves as genuine 'customers'.

While these arguments are all valid, they may equally be applied to the 'purchaser–provider' split. Unless the purchasing authority finds a way to base its purchasing decisions on the views of informed users and some explicit values; unless it consciously shapes the market so that there is a premium on innovation and diversity; unless it invests in gathering and disseminating information; unless it addresses strategic issues that fall outside the immediate remit of social services; and unless it funds genuine advocacy for users – then the mismatch between what people need and the services they get is unlikely to be reduced.

It is an empirical question whether direct user choice or 'proxy' purchasing by the local authority will produce the better match in a particular context, but the prospect of users exercising greater power over the allocation of resources does not generally appeal either to professionals or providers. The current trend is for purchasers to make their lives and budgets simpler by concentrating contracts for services on large, well- established providers and well-tried models. This may encourage replication of good practice; it may equally perpetuate current anomalies, with large chunks of money and people tied up in models that are already dated.

Incompetent communities

Some writers and thinkers offer a still wider interpretation of 'the problem'. They see the problem as the society that generates the need for services, rather than the services themselves. Social oppression, based on negative views of older people (McEwen, 1990) and people with a disability, creates and reinforces dependency; traditional services, controlled by non-disabled people, often make things worse rather than better.

This is not a single school of thought, but a range of perspectives. Writers like Mike Oliver (1990) argue that the disability movement has to combine self-help with wider political activity, as part of a process of 'eradicating the social restrictions and oppressions of disability. Anti-discrimination legislation and a reasonable disability income may contribute to the process, but are not the primary goal of the movement'.

Writers like Connie Lyle and John O'Brien (1988), Judith Snow

13

(1987), Bob Perske (1988) and John McKnight (undated) emphasise that communities that exclude people with disabilities are impoverished and incompetent. They see change in terms of personal relationships and re integrating 'services' with ordinary life. This perspective weaves together elements of Freire (1972) and Illich (1975) with the direct experience of people with disabilities and with the critique of human services developed by Wolfensberger and his followers. 'Normalization', which in its earlier formulations (Bank-Mikkelson, 1969) was primarily a strategy for fixing the disabled person to conform better with social norms, has evolved into 'social role valorisation' (Wolfensberger, 1983), which concentrates on changing the roles society offers to people with disabilities.

This fourth version of 'the problem' is strongly critical of the 'human service machine', not just particular services. The machine is seen as sucking people in and making them into clients rather than helping them get on with their lives 'out there'.

Proponents argue for a transformation rather than a repackaging of services. The focus should be not to 'fix' people who are disabled, but rather to change society so that people with disabilities can live as equal citizens.

Conclusion – signs of progress?

On a narrow view of the problem, success will be easier to manage. Are public funds for residential care being focused more closely on people for whom there is no alternative? Is there a clearer division of responsibilities between agencies in the context of a joint plan for services? These organizational changes are achievable, although they may not lead to a significantly better quality of life for users.

Those who take a wider view of the need for change will be looking for different straws in the wind. They will look for the emergence of new types of service that seek specifically to support integration and inclusion by strengthening 'ordinary' community facilities and services. They will look for improved and destigmatized access to services; better information and clearer rights for service users; the closure of long-stay institutions; and a widespread commitment to quality in service provisions. They will expect the language used about people with disabilities to change, as part of a cultural shift away from charity and towards rights; more court cases initiated by users and users organizations; people with disabilities exercising genuine power in the planning and management of services; changes in the welfare benefits system designed to reduce clienthood. They will expect people with disabilities to be more visible – at work, at school, as part of social and organizational networks.

If these things are happening, the old hierarchical structures will continue to come under pressure and new organizational forms will replace them (Handy, 1989). More professionals will become self-employed, and work on a contract basis for one or more agencies. New agencies such as user co-operatives and community businesses will emerge. Training courses will struggle to keep up with practice. Change and uncertainty will be the rule rather than the exception for a good few years yet.

It is still too soon to say how much real life will change for the people who use or need community care services. The postponement of the financial changes from 1991 to 1993 has prolonged the window of opportunity. But the last 30 years suggest that as a society our commitment to exclusion of people with disabilities is as enduring as our rhetoric.

2 On the receiving end – elderly consumers' perceptions of community care *Ian Sinclair*

Introduction

This chapter is about the reactions of elderly consumers to community care. Its focus is on what elderly people and their carers like or dislike about domiciliary social services and on a policy that aims to keep elderly people out of residential care. Wider definitions of community care and the wider issues relevant to it – the role of the social security and tax systems for example – will be largely ignored and the chapter works within the view of community care implicit in recent government policy. Nevertheless an account of elderly people's views of community care has to take account of some general points about its context. For our purposes three points are particularly relevant.

First, it is important to set any discussion of services against a background of the difficulties and priorities of elderly people themselves. Any discussion of the advantages and disadvantages of a service needs to address the issue of how far this service is central to the concerns of the recipients.

Second, we cannot ignore the issue of resources. It is important to be mindful of Sherlock Holmes' comment about the dog that did not bark in the night. The fact that many frail elderly people have little experience of services may be as important as the experience of services of those that receive them.

Third, we cannot entirely ignore issues of effectiveness. Favourable opinions of services are not the only criteria for judging them. I may, for example, be very pleased with a sympathetic and caring doctor unaware that crucial symptoms have been missed which put me in danger of a serious medical emergency.

The aim of the chapter therefore is to appraise domiciliary services for old people taking account of their priorities and difficulties, consumer opinions and the coverage and effectiveness of the services themselves.

Before continuing a brief explanation is owed to the reader. The original draft of this article contained over two thousand words in references. These have been replaced by reference to two literature reviews by the author. This change was made to achieve the strict word limit rather than from a conscious desire for publicity.

The context of domiciliary services for elderly people

The things elderly people enjoy are various (see, for example, Hunt, 1978; Age Concern, 1974) and so too are their concerns and worries. Important areas of concern are the upkeep of the house and garden, loneliness, and loss of people they have loved (Age Concern, 1974; Hunt, 1978; Jones et al. 1985; Karn, 1977; Shanas et al. 1968; Taylor, 1988; Tunstall, 1957; Wenger, 1984). Undoubtedly much of the unhappiness among elderly people stems from bereavement and disability, two conditions whose incidence obviously increases with age and which have the effect of making it impossible for elderly people to continue the activities and relationships they have previously enjoyed. The effects of bereavement and ill health or disability are recurring threads in studies of morale and depression among elderly people (see, for example, Shanas, 1968; Murphy, 1982).

It is important that most elderly people are not able to do much about spending their way out of these difficulties. In 1986 around two-thirds of those living alone and just under half of those living with someone else had incomes at or below 140 per cent of the state pension (see, for example, Sinclair et al. 1990). A consequence of this lack of money is that given the choice themselves, elderly people seem to spend money on food, clothing and heat rather than on services. Asked how they would spend an unexpected windfall of £200, elderly pensioners thought of home improvements, saving for future emergencies, presents and a variety of other uses, but less than three per cent mentioned services (Martin and White, 1988). Actual expenditure on services by disabled people is also very low (Martin and White, 1988), although expenditure on services rises rapidly with income – in 1986 a pensioner on £125 a week or more spent 39 per cent more on food

17

than one on £45 a week or less but 320 per cent more on services (DE, 1987).

One reason no doubt for the lack of personal expenditure on services is that sums of money available to most elderly people are simply inadequate to make a realistic contribution towards their needs for them – a situation which in the author's view is unlikely to be rectified by new schemes involving insurance and/or the release of housing equity. At present most services for very disabled elderly people are paid for by the state – only in relation to residential care where cash is available from the sale of houses does private income or capital make a sizeable contribution – and in providing services the state necessarily has an eye to costs as well as the wishes of the recipient. More generally it may be spending money on services when in the first instance many elderly people would like more money on the basic pension, which they can spend as they wish.

In place of money, elderly people rely for the solution of their difficulties on drawing in their horns, demonstrating remarkable ingenuity and independence, and receiving help from caring relatives and, to a lesser extent, neighbours. The way they cope is a testament to the resilience of the human spirit and a source of considerable emotional costs to themselves and others. Nearly blind old people may test whether their gas cookers are alight with their hands, acquiring severe burns; severely disabled old people may restrict themselves to one room, living with the stench of a commode; and the incontinent may withdraw from contact with friends (McGrother et al. 1987; Neill et al. 1988).

Relatives caring for old people may also face difficulties from the sheer physical strain of caring, the emotional impact of difficult behaviour or a depressed, apparently ungrateful response, and the conflicts between caring and their social life, family and work (see, for example, Bebbington, 1986; Gilhooly, 1984; Gilleard, 1984; Isaacs et al. 1972; Levin et al, 1989; Lewis and Meredith, 1988; Nissel and Bonnerjea, 1982; Parker, 1985; Sheldon, 1948; Twigg, 1987; Ungerson, 1987; Wright, 1986). Sadly the tasks and strains of caring can erode the emotional basis on which caring is built. It has been estimated that in Great Britain over 400,000 people consider themselves under stress because they provide care for at least 20 hours a week to an elderly person and that 60,000 consider this stress to be unbearable (Sinclair et al. 1990).

The difficulties of poverty, ill health and loss are associated with each

18

other, with age, and with housing. Older generations of old people entered retirement with a poorer standard of living and housing than younger pensioners, and with the passing years their houses and consumer goods deteriorate and such occupational pensions as they may have erode through inflation or the effects of bereavement. Age may add loss, disability and mental impairment to their difficulties, so that the disadvantages of old age fall unequally among pensioners, a process exacerbated by the inequalities already experienced by women, disabled people, black people and manual workers. These accumulated difficulties tend to have a greater effect together than on their own. For example, the likelihood of malnutrition or hypothermia appear to be more increased by a combination of low income and other factors than the factors themselves would lead one to expect (DHSS, 1972; Wicks, 1978).

Despite the very considerable stresses consequent on caring or being in need of care, the great majority of carers and the majority of frail old people do not see residential care as a solution to their difficulties (Campbell et al. 1981; Levin et al. 1989; Salvage, 1986). There is perhaps an exception to this trend in relation to dementia, where the general public at least appears much more prepared than relatives actually caring for the mentally infirm to consider residential care an appropriate solution (West, 1984; West et al. 1984). In general, however, the preference is for care at home, a process seen to require some sacrifice on the part of relatives but not too much. Few, for example, feel that it should entail a daughter giving up work (Salvage, 1986). As far as the general public is concerned, these matters are probably best arranged by local care involving a partnership between state and family (West et al. 1984) and, where necessary, use of sheltered housing (Abrams, 1978; Thompson and West, 1984).

So far, therefore, our discussion of issues in community care would suggest that a policy that set out to meet the aspirations of elderly people would:

- seek to meet the needs of elderly people for cash and reasonable housing at least to the level where, left to their own devices, they would begin to spend money on services
- aim to keep elderly people out of residential care through a partnership between services and families that does not impose too great a burden on the latter
- support elderly people's own determination to maintain their independence

19

● provide services logically related to the consequences of bereavement and disability and to the practical, social and emotional consequences of caring.

In tackling this agenda services face conflicts of priorities that have in part to do with different interests among old people themselves. Concerns about untidy gardens and unkempt houses, for example, are very widespread among old people, but it is difficult to meet these demands while at the same time responding to the needs of carers and of very frail old people on the verge of residential care. There are also conflicts of interest between agencies that aim to help old people. Thus, economies in parts of the public sector (for example, a failure to ensure that old people have centrally heated houses or enough money to buy minimal domestic help) create demands on services. In coal mining areas, for example, home helps may have to make frequent visits to houses of people who are not very frail, simply in order to make sure the fires are going.

It follows from the above that any appraisal of services in the light of old people's views is in part an exercise in priorities, the views of some old people or carers are likely to be given greater priority than those of others. It is also implicitly an appraisal of other parts of the welfare system.

Services and the experience of elderly people

This section concentrates on organized domiciliary services for elderly people and, hence, implicitly on services provided by the state. For although voluntary and private services make a sizeable and perhaps growing contribution to this field (particularly in the areas of meals on wheels, visiting schemes, and nursing agencies), this contribution has not been the subject of much research and is currently dwarfed by the statutory sector. In this respect organized domiciliary services contrast with residential care and sheltered housing for elderly people and unorganized domestic help, areas in which the so-called independent sector is of major importance.

Viewed in the light of the agenda set out in the previous section, the contribution of the statutory sector has both advantages and defects. On the positive side most elderly people and their carers seem to prefer community care to residential care. Moreover, as we will see later, the services received are generally appreciated. On the less positive side, as we have seen earlier, state pensions are not adequate to enable most elderly people to arrange to meet their 'low level' service needs (for example, for domestic cleaning) for themselves. Other defects include:

- a failure to operate a successful policy for keeping people out of residential care (most residents seem to enter at the suggestion of someone else, when they do not really wish to go in and are not so frail that they could not survive in the community without the 24 hour care available in a home, and when they have not been receiving heavy packages of services) (see references in Sinclair et al. 1990, particularly pp.206, 211, 214)
- a failure to support efforts at independence (as evidenced by the lack of occupational therapists in local authorities, particularly in certain parts of the country, defects in the supply and maintenance of aids and adaptations, and a concentration by services on doing what people cannot do rather than helping them to increase their effectiveness) (for example, Bowling, 1987; Clarke et al. 1982; George et al. 1988)
- a failure to support carers who typically receive few, if any, services and whose mental health would in many cases be improved by the removal or death of the person for whom they care (Challis et al. 1988; Gibbins, 1986; Levin et al. 1989; Whittick, 1985)
- a lack of concern with bereavement.

It is important that these defects stem in most cases from lack of resources rather than from inherent problems in the services themselves. Evidence from the Kent Community Care Project and its replication in Gateshead suggests that a sensibly co-ordinated package of services can keep elderly people out of residential care (Challis and Davies, 1986; Challis et al. 1988). Packages of services can minimise, if not necessarily eliminate, the advantage to carers' mental health of their dependent's death or admission to a residential home. The difficulties of responding to bereavement, supporting efforts at independence and taking account of elderly people's varying wishes are more that these take time, trouble and resources than that there is no sense of how to do this. The fact is that given shortage of resources, services have responded by relying on carers and the independence of old people, ignoring emotional concerns with loneliness and bereavement, providing a low level service to as many people as possible, and responding to extreme emergencies with residential care. This is an agenda hardly in keeping with what we know about the priorities of elderly people and their carers.

That said, the services that are received are by and large perceived as relevant and helpful. Such evidence might perhaps be received with scepticism for, as is well known, few people are prepared to say they are dissatisfied with a free service and old people in particular may be reluctant to complain. Certainly more probing styles of interview may reduce apparent degrees of satisfaction with meals on wheels and social work. Nevertheless, at least 50 per cent of elderly people in a study of meals on wheels spontaneously said that the food was 'good' or 'very good' (Johnson et al. 1981) and while such spontaneous expressions of satisfaction with social work may be lower (e.g. Sinclair et al. 1988) the amount of dissatisfaction with social work seems to be lower still (Sinclair et al. 1988). Consumer studies of other services such as home care generally leave little doubt that the services are highly appreciated:

- home helps are appreciated for their efficiency in getting the task done, for the friendliness and company they provide and (by carers) because they allow the carer to get out, or relieve anxiety by visiting an elderly person on their own (Bebbington et al. 1986; Bulmer, 1986; Latto, 1982; Gwynned, 1977; Levin et al. 1989; Sinclair et al. 1988)
- district nurses are valued for the advice they give, their expert help (for example with injections) and the relief they provide from embarrassing or exhausting tasks (Blaxter, 1976; Levin et al. 1989; Sinclair et al. 1988; Wade et al. 1983; Wright, 1986)
- day care is valued for the company and food it provides (Brocklehurst and Tucker, 1980; Carter, 1981; Fennel et al. 1981) and (by carers) for the chance it provides for relatives to get on with their own affairs, for the sense that the load is shared and, sometimes, for the apparent benefits for the elderly person (Levin et al. 1989)
- evidence on other services, such as occupational therapy, voluntary visiting, peripatetic wardens, alarm schemes, care attendants, or relief care is less extensive but gives no grounds for thinking that these services too are not highly appreciated by those who use them (for references seen Sinclair et al. 1990).

It would, of course, be disingenuous to ignore the fact that services are received by those who are prepared to receive them. Day care and relief care, in particular, may be refused by sizeable numbers of people. Moreover, even those receiving services may criticise them for reasons that have to do with poor practice on the part of providers. Home helps, for example, may be criticised because they come late and leave early, because they fail to wait by the door for the old person to come to let them in, because they gossip, smoke and fail to do their work thoroughly, and because they fail to get exactly what the old person wants or respect the way the old person want things done, or to put things in their usual place (see, for example, Sinclair et al. 1988). Similarly day centres may have unstimulating programmes or fail to keep relatives in touch with assessments made of an old person or warn them when the transport cannot come. Such things can be rectified without great expenditure of resources and should be.

That said, many of the criticisms made of services can again be laid at the door of lack of resources. Complaints from recipients and carers about district nurses focus on the difficulty of getting the service in the first place, poor time-keeping, rushed bathing with the old person left undried, and infrequent visits (Bowling and Cartwright, 1982; Levin et al, 1989; Sinclair et al. 1988) – all matters that probably reflect the lack of time available to nurses more than lack of concern or inefficiency on their part. Similar explanations may well apply to complaints about transport to day care, the rushed delivery of meals on wheels, and the low salience of social workers to many frail old people (Sinclair et al. 1988).

Conclusions

The conclusions of this very brief enquiry into consumer views of community care for old people are simple.

On the credit side, the policy of keeping old people out of residential care if at all possible is in keeping with the expressed wishes of most old people and their carers. The services provided to help with this job are, by and large, appreciated and relevant. Adequately resourced and properly co-ordinated services can keep elderly people out of residential care without too much strain on themselves or their carers, which is what all concerned seem to want.

There are also some less encouraging lessons from research. In some cases services could be more sensitively provided and attention to what the consumers think in these cases would be beneficial. The main criticism, however, is that services are simply insufficiently resourced for the job that they have to do. As a result, they are thinly spread over a large number of recipients, carers become exhausted, old people's efforts at independence are unsupported, and too many old people face a choice between residential care, which they do not want, or a depressing struggle that exhausts themselves or their carers. In the context of this lack of resources it is not possible to serve adequately the needs of carers, moderately frail, and very frail old people, nor to give too much weight to the question of what elderly people want.

A solution to these dilemmas requires not so much new ideas, as political will. If pensions and housing were at a level at which frail old people could cater for many of their needs, the task of concentrating services on very frail old people would be easier. If services were adequately resourced, this task could be effectively accomplished. The lessons for the development of community care are therefore clear. So too are the likely consequences for frail old people and their carers if these lessons are not heeded.

3 *At risk and in the community* Susan Hunter and Bill Whyte

The end of the twentieth century is an era characterized by improved standards of living and public health, by advances in medicine and pharmacology and by changing expectations of citizenship and minority rights. For some, this has meant living longer and 'better' lives and, for others, the chance to exchange marginalized institutional living for life in mainstream society. Such major achievements are a cause for celebration and herald a more civilized way of life for us all. In the midst of optimism and opportunity, however, there is a need for caution and concern for vulnerable adults whose 'life in the community' may offer them the 'dignity of risk' (Perske, 1978) but also exposes them to significant dangers. In this paper we ask who are the adults at risk, why might they be considered at risk, why do developments in community care highlight this issue, and what needs to change in order to meet the service challenge and consumer expectations?

Community care: philosophy and policy

The philosophy of normalization (Wolfensberger, 1972) has been a powerful factor in shaping services during the last two decades and in providing the theoretical and moral rationale underpinning the community care legislation. Its assertion of the rights of individuals to life in the mainstream and to services that support this right in a proactive and respectful way is echoed in the aspirations of community care.

The new legislation seeks to achieve changes in the delivery of care services and funding arrangements by emphasizing the enabling rather than providing function of local authorities, by promoting a flourishing

25

independent sector, by enhanced monitoring of cost effectiveness and quality, and possibly by introducing case management. These are radical changes that will alter the face of social work practice.

Of greater pertinence to the focus of this chapter, however, is the legislation's broader aspiration towards enabling people to 'live as normal a life as possible in their own homes or in a homely environment in the community' (HMSO, 1989). To this end, local authorities are required to 'target' those in 'greatest need', to intervene 'no more than is necessary to foster independence', to respond 'flexibly and sensitively' and provide a 'range of options for consumers' including practical support for carers. Successful provision of a range of least-restrictive options in a flexible, user-friendly way to the most vulnerable adults will require services to address considerations of participation, choice, partnership and risk-taking. These activities will require users to have access to information, to be able to understand the information and agree to participate. Where vulnerable adults are not able to understand or participate in these processes, services will require systems that protect the individual's right to take risks and support workers in taking informed risks on behalf of others.

Vulnerable adults and being 'at risk'

Under community care legislation, local authorities will have responsibility for establishing need within their area and for developing plans to meet those needs. It is very difficult to be accurate about numbers in need in a given location and even more difficult to make accurate assessments of need. However, we do know that as a result of the policies and technical advances described, there will be an increasing number of vulnerable adults living in the community. It is well documented (HMSO, 1991) that there will be increasing numbers of people over the age of 85, of people with learning disabilities surviving into old age, of people with severe and chronic mental disorder living in the community, all of whom will have increased support needs seeking services from a changing formal sector. Additionally, it is likely that patterns of divorce and remarriage and an increase in the proportion of women in paid employment will lead to a reduction in the availability of carers in the prime carer generating group, women between 45 and 59 years, resulting in a diminishing or ageing pool of carers from the informal sector (Evandrou, 1990).

Vulnerable adults can be defined as those with some type of physical, emotional or cognitive impairment. They often have special needs and are reliant on others to meet these needs. Health and social care systems can be complex, confusing and difficult to access without assistance. Such dependence of itself, whether on family, friends or service staff, can create vulnerability, leaving them susceptible to indifference, neglect or abuse. Problems of communication and of 'being heard' as a consequence either of the disability itself or ensuing social isolation and lack of opportunity, augments the vulnerability. Motives for discounting the views and desires of vulnerable adults are usually benign; professionals and care-givers see themselves as acting in the 'best interests' of individuals. For adults capable of expressing their views and making choices, such erosion of their self-determination increases their vulnerability and reliance on others. This process is often self-fulfilling, resulting in reduced self-esteem. The impact of this process on, for example, the capacity of institutionalized adults to control even basic aspects of their lives, can be particularly devastating.

Not all vulnerable adults are 'at risk' of neglect, exploitation or abuse. Nonetheless, whether due to physical or mental deterioration, vulnerable adults do sometimes refuse vitally needed services and pose a major problem to professionals attempting to intervene (Aronson, 1983). Irrespective of the efforts of carers and professionals, some vulnerable adults will choose to live in hazardous circumstances and this choice is an informed one; supporting self-determination is a critical professional task. Particular legal and ethical problems are posed for carers and service providers where there is doubt about the level of understanding and insight of the individual taking such a decision. Social work literature continues to lack any clear or practical guidelines in determining when a client should be the involuntary recipient of services or not and whether decisions are indeed in 'the best interests' of the person involved.

Competence, choice and community care

The distinction between 'vulnerability' in which the 'quality of the decision is irrelevant as long as the person understands what he is deciding' and the 'competence to decide' based on mental state is often neither clear-cut nor self-evident (HMSO, 1991, p.20). The law, despite advances in our understanding of mental disorder, generally retains the concept of mental incompetency as an absolute reality; there is no factual basis underlying such an all or nothing view. It is not a discrete state that one is either in or not in; there are gradations of competence, which can vary over time and cannot be abstracted from the demands of particular situations.

Any consideration of the characteristics of these adult groupings and their differential needs highlights this subtlety. The condition of **people with dementia,** for example, is a deteriorating one requiring services that will support them in the community and be capable of adjusting to the increasing and changing demands of the condition. In marked contrast, **people with learning disabilities** face developmental hurdles that require opportunities to maximise control over their own lives. **People with chronic mental illness** often have fluctuating needs; at times access to medication and social support might help them improve their social functioning; at times of relapse or crises more directive involvement may be needed if they are to be maintained in the community and avoid compulsory action (Whyte and Hunter, 1989). The rationale underpinning our moral and legal code is that individuals are entitled to exercise all their rights as citizens including those of physical integrity, but it requires a degree of participation in decision-making to do so. Who then should make the choice on behalf of adults with limited, fluctuating or deteriorating capacities to make choices and take decisions on their own behalf?

The tradition in the Western world has been to follow such adults through the appointment of substitute decision-makers such as guardians, who have the mental capacity and whose decisions may bind persons who lack the mental capacity in their legal relations with the rest of the world (McLaughlin, 1977).

The primary purpose of having a substitute decision-maker from this perspective is to facilitate legally enforceable consent. Protection, however, is seen as a concomitant and important aspect of substitute decision-making, ensuring that responsibility is assumed for monitoring situations to prevent abuse and exploitation. Community care will inevitably place professionals in the role of arbiters of finely balanced decisions about curtailing freedoms and taking calculated risks with little guidance and few safeguards for themselves or their clients. This involves the difficult notion of being 'controlled in one's own best interests'. This control function raises some of the most difficult problems and issues in relation to substitute decision- making as the opportunities for abuse are extensive.

Protecting adults at risk and community care

How realistic is it to talk of protecting adults at risk? Though there can never be an ultimate guarantee, what changes in policy and practice will be required to ensure that adults at risk in the community have a quality of life that would be acceptable to the rest of us?

Some people will always lack the personal relationships, social work and health services, and positive attitudes needed for their protection. No laws, no human services can ensure such things. The problem is too deeply rooted to be solved by law reform alone, by social work departments or by any other 'technological means'. Society cannot legislate the positive attitudes and human relationships that must underlie effective protection. A model of adult protection in community care will have little impact if it is unsupported by a number of other societal developments.

McLauglin (1977) has identified key elements of a broad approach as:

● increased independence of adults at risk
● development of more extensive informal social supports
● increased use of normal social protection mechanisms
● law reform
● development of better planned, more comprehensive, co-ordinated service systems
● development of new protective mechanisms for adults.

Detailed discussion of the first four points is beyond the scope of this paper, which is concerned primarily with changes in the last three areas of legal reform, new protective mechanisms and improving services through community care.

Law reform

Many Western countries have been reviewing their legislative frameworks in the light of community care approaches to service provision for people with mental disabilities (Fram Report, 1987). Useful discussion of these developments in Alberta and Ontario, Canada and in New Zealand are to be found in recent publications by the Scottish Law Commission (1991).

It is our view that the Scottish legislation (in common with all UK provision) has major shortcomings (Whyte and Hunter, 1992). Much of the legislative powers deal only with property and estates (curator bonis powers of attorney) and those that deal with powers over the person are either very inflexible (guardianship) or antiquated (tutors-dative or tutors-at-law). It is a measure of the fragmentation of legal provisions and their inadaptability to the diversity of need and circumstance of adults at risk that local authorities are reluctant to use the powers and that resort has been made in recent years to provisions dating back to 1587 and 1707! (Nichols, 1991).

Although the legislation dealing with guardianship recognizes the potential role in substitute decision-making of supportive family members, particularly 'the nearest relative', our research indicates that this is seldom formally sanctioned (Whyte and Hunter, 1992). For most individuals who lose mental capacity, family and friends often carry the role of de facto substitute deciders without a mandate. However, a public safety net is required for those who do not have supportive relatives or friends to whom they can turn for personal decisions in such an event. Equally there is a need for legislative provision that allows people to determine all aspects of their life in advance of their becoming mentally incapacitated.

New provisions encompassing both financial stewardship and personal guardianship in a flexible framework are clearly required and are currently under consideration north and south of the border (HMSO, 1991a, 1991b). They must take account of the differential needs of the client groups involved; the so-called Commonwealth model offers one way forward, allowing for a **menu** of powers that can be **selected** to meet a **specified need** in an individual and **varied** as the need changes.

Protective mechanisms

Theoretically available to all citizens, the normal protective mechanisms of the law, the courts, the press etc., are used less effectively on behalf of adults at risk. Advocacy has developed as an important response to this difficulty within human services. It is now a familiar concept in social work literature but suffers from a diversity of interpretation; various forms have emerged including citizen, self and agency advocacy.

Social workers tend to see good social work practice as synonymous with advocacy. Wolfensberger contends, and we would agree, that social work is not always the same as advocacy. There can be an unavoidable conflict between the interests of the social worker as an employee of a public agency, and the interests of the client. When a social worker is caught between legitimate but incompatible demands, advocacy on behalf of the client is likely to suffer. For this reason Wolfensberger puts particular reliance on volunteers to carry out social advocacy. In pointing out the weakness of using social service workers for advocacy, he does not deny they have an important role in protecting adults at risk. That role, however, is through protective services not as long-term advocates.

These distinctions are particularly relevant to the implementation of community care. As care manager, directed by a needs-led or consumer-led assessment, the social worker may well have an important advocacy function in ensuring the agreed package of care is delivered. However, as care manager responsible for the rational use of limited resources, the conflict of interest identified by Wolfensberger is equally likely to arise. The centrality of the purchaser–provider split in managing such conflicts is underlined in this context.

Some would go further and suggest that a system of independent accountability is necessary to free professionals in making assessments from the conflicts of interest likely to be inherent in their roles, especially that of lead agency employees. In this context, even the provision in the Tom Clarke Bill (Disabled Persons Act, 1986) for an 'authorised representative' remains circumscribed as well as unimplemented, though the attribution of legislative status to the concept of citizen advocacy would have been an important step forward.

Scotland already possesses a unique system that attempts to reconcile such tensions with regard to decision-making for children. The Children's Hearing System with its lay panels is highly regarded and arguably highly effective. McCreadie (1989) has already argued that a similar system for adults at risk would provide an appropriate arena to have the needs of such adults 'heard' and responded to. In addition, it would provide an external control over decision-making and hold service providers, and in particular any appointed guardians (or formally mandated persons), to account for their actions. A system modelled on the hearing system, able to provide external control over decision-making and use of resources as well as draw on community wisdom, differing professional expertise and the knowledge of carers, could provide a robust plank in the foundations for quality community care, while freeing the court to deal with the necessary adjudication and adversarial issues.

Whatever the system of decision-making and accountability, the differential needs of the client groups involved can only be met in a legislative frame that allows for change and flexibility in the use of compulsory powers.

Better human services and community care

The work of Wolfensberger and others points to the segregation of disabled persons into specialized and institutionalized services as major stigmatizing processes. The use of culturally normative approaches to meeting need and the integration of clients into ordinary human service patterns, rather than segregation, are keystones in service planning and delivery under community care legislation. If adequate community services are developed, specialized involuntary protection services like guardianship, should be needed rarely.

However, it is not just a matter of resources; professional practice will have to shift gear to meet the demands of the community care legislation. Apart from the well discussed question of developing needs-led rather than resouce-led assessments, many professionals, but especially lead-agency ones, will have to refocus their assessments away from institutional processing (Samuel et al. 1992) towards community care planning with a particular emphasis on frameworks for risk assessment.

Social workers are well versed in risk-assessment, particularly in relation to children, but the legal and attitudinal framework in relation to adults at risk increases the complexity and ambiguity of the task. In a previous study (Whyte and Hunter, 1992) it seemed to us that social workers' natural inclination was towards assessing the level of risk *per se* and the need for social services rather than social indicators of client mental capacity to make decisions on their own behalf. Indeed once a client settled, having been institutionalized involuntarily, some workers no longer saw the relevance of guardianship, even though there was no evidence of improvement in mental competence. In the world of community care, the opportunities for sheltering under the reassuring umbrella of the residential resource and for operating a collective model of decision-making will be reduced. Even if improved interdisciplinary team working steps into the breach, the professionals will require greater clarity and confidence in reaching decisions independent of resource availability.

Attaching greater status and priority in practice to this area of work and more investment in training, is undoubtedly part of the solution. However individuals are unlikely to practice the kind of informed risk-taking that will be required to meet the expectations of the legislation and the consumer without the parallel development of a risk-taking culture within services. Management will have to devise structures that enable and support workers to take informed risks; otherwise flexibility, innovation and effort to meet consumer wishes will be overwhelmed by the rigid and bureaucratic strategies that have begun to characterize the child protection field. Whilst the ADSW initiative (1990) in this area is a welcome one, the emergence of practice guideline preoccupied primarily with 'covering' agencies, would not be.

Conclusion

As a consequence of the improved social conditions described earlier, reinforced by the social policies of community care, there are increasing numbers of vulnerable adults living in the community who are likely to be at risk of exploitation, abuse, neglect or exclusion from decision-making because of, among other things, reduced mental capacity.

The introduction and implementation of community care planning for this particular group means meeting service delivery expectations without an adequate legal, administrative or practice infrastructure, which really is putting the cart before the horse. It is a matter of urgency that a legal framework be elaborated that allows individuals to make decisions in advance of reduced mental capacity; that a reliable infrastructure of facilitative services is evolved that helps people to be heard and ensures the use of compulsion only as a last resort; that adequate systems of accountability are instituted to safeguard those for whom others are empowered to make decisions, especially where conflict of interest occurs.

4 Care or neglect in the care of the community? Naina Patel

Introduction

Excerpt from the *Daily News* 2 April 1992:

'Yesterday, 1 April 1992, was the deadline for local authorities to submit their community care plans to the Minister. Social services throughout the country, along with health authorities, in consultation with voluntary and private organizations – not to forget the wider public – have produced plans to ensure that community care services are in place (for implementation in 1993) to aid people at crucial juncture. The key objective is to make sure that users live in the community as independently as possible. Flexibility, choice, users' and carers' involvement are some of the overriding concerns of this new policy as is the intention to consult with minority groups in putting together purchasing strategy. This latter emphasis follows from the 1989 White Paper, *Caring for People* (DOH, 1989), which highlighted the particular needs of people from ethnic minorities,

"the Government recognizes that people from different cultural backgrounds have particular care needs and problems. Minority communities may have different concepts of community care and it is important that service providers are sensitive to these variations. Good community care will take account of the circumstances of minority communities and will be planned in consultation with them". (2.9 pp.10–11)

In accordance with these requirements, as now set in the NHS and Community Care Act 1990, the authorities in the process of submitting their community care plans took the challenge of meeting minority needs *seriously* in their planning design and development of services for black people – *News Reporter.*'

34

The black reality and community care

In reality, however, 1 April was indeed 'April Fools' Day' for many authorities and black groups! So it will be for the implementation of community care to begin on 1 April 1993. Over the last two years the care sector has generally been characterized by staff working themselves to a point of exhaustion in order to master the legislation (including the Children's Act, 1989), to put the community care plans together, to write the guidance papers and endless reports and, time permitting, to gather further documentation from other quarters. Many staff had hoped that after the deadline for submission of community care plans, a hung parliament might be returned allowing at least some time to read all the papers, guidance documents, etc. This was wishful thinking. In the post-election environment of fundamental change, as envisaged by the community care legislation, consider the plight of individuals and communities who are through discrimination and disadvantage relegated to the margins of society (blacks, disabled and poor people, etc.). At the best of times, information provision and action are regarded as poor to such groups. In Britain today matters are getting worse.

Given the general shrinkage in resources and chaos in welfare services, many black community organizations have not heard or fully understood the implications of proposed plans for community care let alone participated in the consultative process. For some, understandably, they were the casualties of central government's poll tax capping (Burdett, 1990) and faced closures as local authorities withdrew or reduced grants. It is necessary to undertake further work in this area to assess the impact of such closures on black communities, given the *primary* role played by black voluntaries.

The scenario posed in the 'report' earlier is therefore far from reality for many individuals and organizations. As for the 57 words on ethnic minorities cited in the legislation, these would only be meaningful to black people if we assumed:

- that well developed services already *exist* – it would then only be a question of *who* provides them[1]
- that service staff have the necessary skills and knowledge to make an appropriate assessment of 'needs' and that these are contextualized within a system acknowledging the existence of racism and poverty so that services are designed, planned, developed and delivered with the appropriate resources

● that the existing information on black people's current usage of mainstream and voluntary services, as well as the number and type of voluntary organizations who support black communities, is sufficient. This information is necessary to build a profile of the 'specific local market' for services and in assessing the potential demand for these in the future.

I shall examine each of the above assumptions to establish the likely effectiveness of the current planning process and consequent implementation of plans, especially regarding the identification of needs of black and minority groups. I shall deal with the first two assumptions simultaneously.

Needs, uptake and mainstream services

Black communities are characterized by ethnic, gender, class, sexuality, disability and health differences. They have expectations and aspirations for an improvement in quality of life no different to white communities. However, racism and poverty experienced in employment, housing, health and education have resulted in the majority of black people occupying a working class position in Britain (Runnymede Trust, 1980; Sivanandan, 1991).

With high levels of unemployment over the last decade, rising poverty has been a fact of life for a significant section of the black community. This is worsened by the fact that state benefits are not fully claimed because of lack of information – or because of complex forms, language difficulties and welfare rules that are not being sufficiently responsive to different household structures (e.g. in extended families, some members may not pay housing cost but will contribute to general expenses). Consequently, black people's needs for welfare services has increased over the last decade given the nature of their social economic position. Yet, as Bhalla and Blakemore (during the early 1980s) and Evers et al (in the late 1980s) show, the existence of day care provision, sheltered housing, meals on wheels and community health services is generally unknown to black elders. Research indicates an increasing usage of such services, once known, when they are appropriate. Nevertheless, some authorities, even in the 1990s, continue to respond unhelpfully when called to make provision for appropriate services for black users. Frequently difficulties are claimed in 'catering for specific

dietary needs' or 'recruiting specific language speaking staff'. Sometimes we are told, 'there is no demand for residential care because
traditional families look after their own' (Moore 1991).

The existence of black self-help projects in the last decade has at least
shown that in the area of welfare services, no *pre-existing* provision from
statutory or traditional voluntary sector existed for black groups
(Norman, 1985; Bowling, 1990). Essentially, it is the black voluntary
sector that has made black people visible and pioneered services
relevant for them. For example, Francis (1991) points out that in
mental health services:

'In spite of the deaths of several young black men in psychiatric hospitals
and prisons (Francis, 1985, 1989), the government has maintained a studied
silence . . . Agencies like the Afro-Carribean Mental Health Association
(ACMHA) and Nafsiyat have pioneered new practices which recognize the
unique social position of black communities in Britain. Nafsiyat makes
psychotherapy available to black clients who are normally considered
linguistically or intellectually incapable of benefiting from psycho-therapy'
(Kareem 1988, p.87, 1991).

However, most such projects are small scale and many exist on
temporary shoestring budgets (Blakemore, 1985; Bowling, 1990; Patel,
1990). Various studies on black voluntaries and elderly people show
that these projects cannot be expected to provide comprehensive
services to *all* black elders in the community. Nor can they reach all
sections such as frail elderly or disabled people. In Bowling's study all
four projects examined shared the problem of short-term funding,
leading him to raise a critical question in his conclusion:

'to what extent is it possible for Central Government, Local Government,
Age Cocnern and other voluntary organizations to retain credibility for their
claims of "commitment" to "helping the community to care" when low-
cost community based initiatives which are up and running, demonstrating
consistent support for elderly people within the community, are allowed to
die through lack of long-term funds?' (p.50)

As to the functions of black voluntary groups, the pressing requirement
to meet the immediate needs of black people explains their proliferation
and diverse roles. Mirza (p.137) illustrates this point in relation to
auditing tasks in community care planning:

'these groups are multi-faceted and do not fit easily into existing models of
social service provision. For example, a group may provide advocacy
services as well as running a club for the elderly and dealing with enquiries

on housing and welfare benefits. The origins and practice of many groups servicing the needs of the black community are rooted in their understanding of the discrimination faced by the black and minority ethnic community and how to combat such discrimination. Audits of a black and minority ethnic voluntary group fail to account sufficiently for these factors and these groups will inevitably suffer if a social audit is undertaken'.

It is thus important to note here the crucial role of the black voluntary sector in the absence of mainstream services: they *are* playing a substitute role not a complementary one as in the traditional voluntary sector. In essence black self-help projects have become the *primary* providers of care. Such projects are often financially supported and positively viewed by mainstream health and social services because they provide a 'buffer' against direct criticism of failure to provide mainstream services. Since they are characterized by small budgets, often on a short term basis, a 'fringe' provision is created, which in a climate of financial stringencies can be trimmed, cut or stopped as shown by Bowling's study. Arguments about autonomy and effectiveness cannot be sustained when such groups are marginalized and functioning on a minimal resource base but are nevertheless simultaneously required to be the *primary* providers of care. Such an arrangemeent simply assigns black users to a peripheral existence, an additional obstacle over and above the general marginalization of black people.

Structurally, black voluntaries are the 'weak' players in any competitive tender to provide for services to black people. It is in this context that black voluntaries will need to be vigilant that:

- they are not required to change or expand their function in a way which organizationally they cannot sustain, despite the consequent attractions of receiving a 'larger share in the market' or improved funding
- they are not squeezed out because their relationship with the purchaser is unequal in terms of size, resources and established infrastructure
- if they are 'forming bridges' with traditional white voluntaries, their relationship is not substituted with the one previously held with the statutory sector. In other words, there are inherent dangers in such an arrangement given the relative strength of the established traditional white voluntary agencies who can determine the terms of the 'partnership', that is an internal colonial system can be built up within the provider relationship of black and white voluntaries working together.

Alternatively, black voluntaries could choose, as many are doing currently, to go for contracts for grant aid instead of contracts for different forms of social care. The former approach allows a greater certainty of funding, independence and autonomous existence particularly since, as discussed earlier (cited Mirza, 1991), black voluntaries are multifunctional. Specializing in one area may well transfer much needed resources to other areas and transform the agency's wider function with the local community. Jones cites just such an example in the Midlands:

> '[an Asian women's group] was set up to deal with violence against Asian women. The women were approached by the local social services authority to put together a contract to provide Asian meals-on-wheels. The group knew Asian elders would benefit and the skills were there to provide the meals. It was a real dilemma. The downside was that this was a completely different function from the one they were set up to perform. It was in fact an extension of local authority services. The women's group felt that their position would be compromised' (cited in Daurado, p.23, *Community Care*, 1991).

The offer from the local social services department was thus rejected.

Market orientation in community care: implications for black voluntaries

Since it is well known that stereotyping, gatekeeping, individual, organizational and direct racism(s) effectively work to keep black people out of the market for welfare services (Patel, 1990), what should black people expect of a care management system that essentially is a gateway into services? What kind of eligibility criteria for a referral to a case manager can ensure that black people do not continue to be disserviced? Given the evidence of great levels of unmet needs of black people (Bhalla and Blakemore, 1981; Patel, 1990; Francis, 1991; Bowling, 1991; Pharoah, 1991; Mirza, 1991), where will the case managers begin in the drawing of individual service plans for the user? In response to requests for services, will the case manager be sufficiently trained with anti-racist knowledge and skills to translate these requests into appropriate services (with client consent) or, with various racist myths operating,[2] will they be *screened out* as inappropriate referrals? Since the current underlying theme of community care is that welfare maximization of individuals is best determined by maximizing individual liberty ('freedom of choice'), minimalist state intervention, to encourage voluntarism within the family and the voluntary sector, is seen as the ideal way of providing care. The endemic nature of racism in British society operationalized by individuals and institutions makes the above question quite central to 'meeting the needs' of black users.

In the 1990s, demographic changes (e.g. the number of black elders is expected to double), increased poverty and continuing unemployment, with little prospect for reflation and recovery following the 1980s restructured and reduced public welfare services[3] mean that there will be an increase in the demand for welfare services. In these circumstances, black workers and black voluntaries will, if they have not already done so, need to equip themselves fully with their local social services community care plans in order to register *changes* where necessary, particularly if they were not consulted in the first instance.

In the community care world of competitive practices, black voluntaries may need to collaborate with each other and to cluster their activities as one provider group with a number of subgroups catering for specific service needs and ethnic groups (if relevant). Apart from large agencies being able to negotiate a better price for services provided, they may well benefit from other economies of scale in development, training, accounting and financial systems – as well as bringing together, as a stronger whole, diverse black groups, subdivided into specific 'ethnic' groups in the 1970s and 1980s through state funding and internal desires of individual communities (Sivanandan, 1991). In the absence of a considerable expansion of resources, local social services will undoubtedly face pressure to go for contracts which show value for money: the experience over the last decade suggests that this usually means low cost services, not necessarily efficient ones which are sensitive to the needs of all users. This attitude therefore will inevitably favour large service providers over smaller ones (Atkin, 1991).

Nevertheless, if smaller black voluntaries were to group together[4] on a larger scale, there is no reason why black voluntaries with their experience of struggles and innovation in services, could not *also* be service providers for white users. Now that would be a real test of purchasers' commitment to a multi- racial society and non-discrimination![5] Nor should we discount the possibility that a black-led private sector may well emerge in the near future: entrepreneurs, black or white, are not so choosey if they can see a market potential to exploit, whether it will be for profits or investment in the community is another matter.

Market information

Returning to the third assumption (see p. 36) on the knowledge of a 'local market' for services, anecdotal evidence suggests that information regarding black groups is uneven and is not fully exchanged within the local authority. Butt's national research (1991) shows confusions and inconsistencies in the use of ethnic record keeping and monitoring of services (ERKM):

> 'What is clear is that SSDs have differing views as to what constitutes an ERKM system. Some have interpreted the ability to record ethnic origin as an ERKM system, while others who do record ethnic origin do not believe they have an ERKM system. In addition, some take account of religion, language and diet while many others do not'.

Explaining why such difficulties have arisen in the implementation of ERKM, Butt offers several reasons:

> 'the failure to carry out any analysis leading to the system being seen as a bureaucratic imposition; the establishment of ERKM system outside an EOP policy for service delivery; viewing ERKM as a mainly strategic tool for aggregate analysis only; lack of clarity as to why information is needed and what information should be recorded. As a result the quality of the information available is adversely affected' (cited in SHARE Newsletter 2, March 1992, p.4).

Intelligence gathering will then be a necessary first task for many social services departments, while others will need to examine the quality of their data collection methodology, as well as the usage of information where it is adequate.

As for carers, since many do not regard themselves as 'carers', apart from raising their expectations concerning entitlements, they will need to be supported with adequate resources (given the low socio-economic backgrounds of many black people). Community care changes have seemingly created a situation where all providers are seen as being in the mainstream. But if the present organizational structure continues with black voluntaries seen by purchasers as being able to meet all the identified needs of black people, then there is no reason to doubt that the overall welfare position of black people will remain a secondary one and marginalization will be reinforced.[6] However, at an individual level user's determination of needs, if these are adequately expressed to a case manager, may well enhance individual welfare and can 'democratize' the service system.

The 'invisible hand' taking care

The community care legislation, however, uses the 'market' as a tool for creating such a dynamic. We know that a need in a market situation does not necessarily translate itself into a demand, if you do not have money to express that demand, nor can the market respond to a need if there is no one to supply it! Mishan (by no means a radical economist) states:

> 'for what they choose freely to buy depends on what is offered to them and on the prices charged . . . neither the full range of feasible opportunities nor the proper costing of existing goods and services can be assumed to emerge from the operation of competitive markets alone. Government initiative has a decisive role to play (*Consumer choice rules the market*, 1971).

It is also necessary to note here that throughout the community care legislation rationality of choice is of paramount importance in determining choices by the user. In the ordinary goods market, this is a problematic concept let alone in the market for welfare services (Patel, 1989).

Conclusion

In conclusion, it is necessary to offer a critique of community care legislation and its particular impact on black people and black voluntaries: its low cost principle ultimately creates a low-wage, low-welfare economy with inadequate expectations for training in the public domain. This critique does not mean that the status quo – with more of the same – would be a better model of welfare. As I have shown elsewhere (Patel, 1990) black older people, for example, have not benefited from the existing system. The critique instead points us to the necessity of using the principles of individual welfare and choice with individual *rights* (instead of needs) which are shared collectively in the society. Pfeffer and Coote (1991) offer an alternative approach to free market thinking and since the introduction of community care met with little debate (see Biggs, 1990) it is essential that their model gains some attention even though community care is going ahead and the political climate is unfavourably certain – at least for the next five years.

I have further suggested that 'being sensitive' and undertaking 'consultation' *are not sufficient* since they exclude the organizational system and those within it. Consultation does not necessarily lead to negotiation or participation in the final outcome of service provision. But as Dutt (1991) argues, black groups organizing collectively can make the 57 words in the White Paper mean something to black people's experience in improving their quality of life.[7] For example, the fact that five established groups of and for Asian people with care needs in London were *not* consulted on community care plans and consequently joined forces to form Asian Community Care Forum is certainly encouraging (Chauhan, 1992). What this shows is that any meaningful and effective outcome for black people is dependent on their taking the lead – a lead that they have taken for some time since community care is not a new concept for these communities in the absence of mainstream services in the UK.

Appendix 1

According to the requirements cited earlier, is being 'sensitive' and 'consulting minorities' sufficient to ensure that necessary services will be provided to black people? Translating these 57 words into action at a local level would mean that:

1. For planning purposes social services departments basic information on:

   (a) the composition of its community by age, 'race', ethnicity, gender, disability, mental health and so on
   (b) existing agencies providing a range of services to black communities, that is, a measurement of supply
   (c) demand for services of users and carers. This raises the question of consultation and participation in determining the nature of services required. How this information about services is translated to communities and how information from communities is translated into services calls into question the kind of information system to be developed and established
   (d) how the agencies reach carers particularly in the system when many see it as their traditional role and do not recognize themselves as carers?

    (e) whether black voluntaries are given information on different funding options: contract for grant aid or contract for social care services?

2. For implementation social services departments would need to:

    (a) analyse their workforce composition as providers or purchasers

    (b) ensure that information on services reaches the actual and potential users and carers in the community, assuming proper consultation and participation methods in the planning process;

    (c) plan for sustaining consultative links so that the service continues to be responsive to demand

    (d) ensure that staff are prepared to be competent in anti-racist practice that also reflects an understanding of diverse cultural, religious and linguistic needs

    (e) ensure that information on individual needs collected by case management systems indicates resource (including workforce type) and service deficits. Given black people's historical unmet need, agencies would need to target the purchasing strategy in this area. So too as purchasers, they would need to work with black groups to write service specifications

    (f) recognize the disadvantageous position of black voluntaries, and provide support to them to prepare tenders and create conditions (including laying down of standards) that enable entry of black voluntaries as new providers in the market for services

    (g) include and monitor other providers' commitment to service black and minority group's needs. In the process of doing this, will agencies have sufficient understanding that black voluntaries are not 'crowded out' by larger traditional providers?

    (h) ensure in 'stimulating the market' that black voluntaries whom they want to provide services are not required to expand overnight or compromise their work and independence.

SECTION TWO:
THE IMPLEMENTATION OF COMMUNITY CARE

(i) Planning the Care

5 *From joint planning to community care planning – some lessons* David Hunter

Over the past year or so health and local authorities across the country, together with voluntary organizations, have been busy producing community care plans as part of the community care reforms being progressively phased in over three years from April 1991. The White Paper *Caring for People* and subsequent guidance from the Department of Health/Social Services Inspectorate (in England) and Social Work Services Inspectorate (in Scotland) are unequivocal in their insistence that interagency co-ordination is crucial to the successful planning and delivery of community care (DOH, 1990: DOH/SSI and Scottish Office Social Work Services Group, 1991). Ministers have stated repeatedly that close working links between all agencies must be firmly in place.

None of this is new. Exhortations by successive governments to encourage collaboration and joint working between agencies have become commonplace. Yet they have fallen short of the desired impact. The record of health and local authority collaboration is not an encouraging one. Official inquiries (e.g. Working Group on Joint Planning, 1985; Audit Commission, 1986; House of Commons Committee of Public Accounts, 1988; Griffiths, 1988; House of Commons Social Services Committee, 1990) and academic research (Glennerster, Korman and Marslen-Wilson, 1983; Hunter and Wistow, 1987; Challis et al. 1988; Hunter and Richards, 1990; Hunter and Wistow, 1991; Wistow, 1990; Wistow and Hardy, 1991) have documented comprehensively the failures and problems in the context of some 15 years' experience of joint planning.

Notwithstanding this catalogue of general failure in collaborative working, there have been some modest successes to which both the Audit Commission and Sir Roy Griffiths pointed in their respective appraisals of community care policy. This suggests that part of the explanation for failure in collaboration has been the unrealistically high expectations for joint planning evident on the part of its architects. If community care planning is not to suffer a similar fate then there are important lessons to be learnt from the experience of joint planning. With this aim in view, this chapter offers an assessment of joint planning and reviews the principal lessons to emerge from it. The hope is that the analysis will inform current practice and will provide some pointers towards the successful implementation of community care planning.

Obstacles

From the history of joint planning it is possible to document numerous obstacles. These have been organized into five categories by Wistow and Hardy (1991): structural, procedural, financial, professional, status and legitimacy. In a comprehensive review of joint planning, a DHSS working group pointed to a series of problems embracing all five categories (Working Group on Joint Planning, 1985). The report commented on a variety of obstacles to joint planning. In particular, it noted the lack of coterminosity between health and local authorities, and problems over the availability of resources, especially bridging finance. Other constraints included: different management structures between local and health authorities, and methods of organization and financial systems; the wide range of services provided by social services departments and their accountability to the local electorate; differences in the pay structures of health and local authorities, which can hamper staff transfers; obstacles stemming from the attitudes and relationships of individuals including: different perceptions of priorities, different professional traditions and perceived status, the innate tendency in all organizations to defend territories and budgets, and the natural concern of staff about the effect of change on jobs.

Joint planning has posed problems where planning generally has appeared to be weak within health authorities and social services departments. Even where strong formal systems of planning have existed they have not precluded the need for informal networks. A pronounced degree of opportunism has existed in arrangements for joint planning with subgroups often being set up as a specific response to a perceived need to act.

Most of what has passed for joint planning is confined to a limited range of services that in most cases does not include housing and education. Too much joint planning, it is suggested, has focused on negotiations between service-providing agencies and on 'tiptoeing through vested interests'.

Problems of organization have also been to the fore in respect of joint planning. They exist principally in the rigid vertical hierarchies evident in health and local authorities, which has made it difficult to establish horizontal working through mechanisms such as joint consultative committees (JCCs) and joint care planning teams (JCPTs). Managerial and professional hierarchies have nearly always defeated attempts to construct more lateral forms of organization. The operation of JCCs and JCPTs has presented major structural and procedural problems. Underlying all of these structural and procedural obstacles has been the great diversity between local government and NHS cultures and structures. The diversity has been most apparent in the area of planning where philosophies have conflicted and planning horizons have been completely different.

Joint finance (support finance in Scotland) or 'collaboration money' as it has been termed, was introduced in the mid-1970s (1980 in Scotland) to pump prime joint planning. Many managers have seen it as the key to effective joint planning. From the evidence, it seems clear that joint finance suffers from two major weaknesses. First, it can divert attention from examining the purposes to which mainstream budgets are put. Second, there is a lack of clarity over what joint finance adds. It can represent a cheap source of capital but since many community care developments do not hinge upon such expenditure this can introduce a bias and distortion in the type of developments receiving support. Most community care developments require long-term revenue funding. Unless local authorities are reconciled in the long run to meeting the revenue costs, then joint finance's appeal is virtually limited to representing a cheap source of capital.

Under the community care planning arrangements, joint finance will continue for a time at least. There is therefore a risk that the distorting effect of joint finance upon collaborative working could continue unless those involved in community care planning confine joint finance to its proper role as a source of pump priming funds to initiate innovative schemes and new developments. It is not a substitute for funding from mainstream budgets.

Inter-professional difficulties and differences are often cited as lying

49

at the centre of problems over communication and effective joint planning. Apart from problems arising from attempts at horizontal communication across agencies, problems of communication vertically within organizations have also been evident in studies of joint planning. Professional defensiveness has served to thwart numerous attempts at collaboration. Notions of status have been important barriers.

Facilitating factors

From the evidence available, joint planning is more likely to succeed when:

- time is invested in it and there is input from all the agencies concerned
- information is produced on existing services and on identifying where the gaps are
- regular reviews of progress are completed as an initiative develops to ensure it stays on the right track
- developments are kept manageable, i.e. small and are not over-ambitious
- working groups prepare the ground and develop proposals
- key workers are appointed
- joint finance is available
- informal relations between agencies are well developed to allow continuity of thought and practice.

Effective joint planning can take time. Whether or not it is successful can hinge upon arriving at an optimal balance between top–down and bottom–up influences. Locality planning is increasingly viewed as a way of bridging the gap between strategic activity on the one hand and operational activity on the other. Collaboration is most likely to succeed if operational objectives are clear before attempts are made to collaborate; if specific areas for collaboration are concentrated on rather than trying to spread activity too thinly; and if enthusiasm is present.

Many of the most successful examples of joint planning have emerged from structural innovations that have bypassed or have only been loosely accountable to joint consultative committees and joint care planning teams. Successful organizational forms have centred on management partnerships, multi-disciplinary teams and other devices that have not only crossed agency and professional boundaries but have also had executive authority delegated to them in order to make more rapid progress in the development of integrated approaches. Within these organizational forms, single joint service managers, case or care managers or key workers have all been important devices to overcome boundary problems of one sort or another.

The importance of enabling structures like common boundaries and particular machinery like JCCs and JCPTs has been limited. They appear to have been unable to secure progress by themselves and should only be seen as an aid to joint planning where there already exists a commitment to such activity. If joint planning is to be anything other than a hit or miss affair then the need for structures of some kind cannot be dismissed out of hand. The important point, however, is that it is the *combination of factors* that seems to be important in securing progress in joint planning and not the existence of any one factor in isolation.

Effective joint planning is dependent upon good inter-relationships between professionals. Where informal relationships between health and local authorities have existed they have led to continuity of planning and to successful initiatives. Such factors were evidenced by several observers as critical to achievements in various schemes. Whereas much of the concern about joint planning has centred on structures, on creating coterminosity, and on achieving the planned organization of service boundaries so as to minimise multiple overlaps, in reality, where mutual trust has existed between senior officers from health and local authorities, the relationship has appeared to be far more important than joint planning machinery.

With all the obstacles arrayed against it, it is a wonder that joint planning succeeds at all. Yet it does. The Audit Commission, in its critique of community care policy, conceded that joint planning could work and cited examples accordingly. One of the problems, however, in assessing whether joint planning has been successful is the lack of hard evidence on effective outcomes. Nevertheless, given the reality described by those who have studied joint planning, the clear message is not to continue the search for an elusive nirvana, but to modify and manipulate the reality that exists in order to make modest but useful progress.

Community care planning: guidelines for practice

Effective inter-agency planning will continue to be an important element in the new framework provided by the White Paper changes.

If policy makers and managers at all levels are serious about overcoming the administrative and professional barriers that serve to inhibit joint planning, and now community care planning, then there needs to be a commitment to learning the lessons from initiatives that have sought to confront these obstacles. Only in this way can well-informed and appropriate structures for joint planning be designed which reflect a true understanding of the pitfalls and of how they might best be avoided or circumnavigated.

Derived from the foregoing review of the evidence in respect of joint planning, the following guidelines for practice in community care planning are put forward for consideration and reflection:

- success is more likely to be forthcoming where a commitment to collaborative working already exists and where there is actual experience of such collaboration upon which to build
- a clearly focused purpose, for which some kind of co-ordinated response is seen as an appropriate solution needs to be identified. Often collaborative working is not directed at a particular objective but is invoked at a general catch-all level. There needs to be agreement on both the nature of the problem and the response to it. This demands an explicit common vision and set of principles to ensure a clear sense of direction. It is all too easy for joint planning and the machinery for undertaking it to become an end in itself rather than a means to an end.
- clear operational objectives stated in advance are less important than a proven capacity to adapt over time as seems necessary, but nevertheless in a way consistent with the strategic vision
- joint planning takes time and requires leadership, commitment and direction from senior management to ensure that it is given sufficient priority within the organization and to enable decisions to be taken promptly without constant referral up the line to parent authorities. Particularly in respect of local authorities, considerable delegated authority to representatives on joint planning groups is an essential prerequisite.
- locality planning and similar devices are an attempt to bridge the gap between strategic planning and operational decision making. Joint plans will not succeed if those on the receiving end of them feel excluded from their production. Hence the importance of attention being devoted to *vertical* joint approaches within agencies as well as *horizontal* ones across them

- *joint planning machinery* is secondary to *joint planning process*. Service managers should have confidence in those individuals who tend to operate on the boundaries of the organization and allow them the space to do so in order to promote collaborative activity. Many successful joint initiatives have proceeded on an opportunistic basis rather than on a rationally planned one. Attempts to change behaviour through institutional or structural devices will usually fail unless concomitant changes have been effected in the structure of advantage, i.e. resource and power dependencies, among those groups inhabiting organizations and seeking to work together
- incentives are important. For some, joint planning and collaborative activity is its own reward. But for many others a lubricant is necessary – perhaps in the form of joint finance or bridging finance – in order to provide an incentive and to make progress. However, such funds are not an incentive to planning if processes designed to foster planning serve to displace this activity into allocating relatively small sums of money
- it is wise to avoid being overambitious. Joint planning seems to work best when discrete, manageable projects or initiatives are undertaken. The aims should be modest in order to secure real progress rather than merely the semblance of change. Unrealistic expectations can only lead to a loss of commitment to joint planning. Co-ordination should not be oversold
- a shared sense of ownership among all interested parties is vital. This means that policy needs to be agreed to and shared by all those involved in its implementation. Too often policies exist as something distinctively separate from practice and are cast in vague, ambivalent terms not particularly relevant or helpful at an operational level, where they lack specificity and come up against often varying professional views of how things ought to be done
- effective collaborative working demands particular skills in view of the often highly sensitive and political nature of the work. The skills are not primarily technical or competency-based but social and interpersonal with a stress on entrepreneurial and networking activity across agency boundaries and professions
- Not all problems are amenable to a solution based on collaborative working. Collaboration is not a panacea for problems whose origins lie in basic funding shortages or in systemic malfunctioning in the care infrastructure

If these guidelines for practice are followed and satisfactorily acted upon, then the chances of community care planning being successful in a particular locality should be greatly enhanced. Nonetheless, what happens locally cannot be entirely divorced from the overall national policy context and it is important that this should be seen as supportive of community care planning rather than as undermining work in this area. Above all, it is important to acknowledge that there is no 'how-to-do-it kit' or manual or cookbook for successful joint planning.

As the evidence reviewed above demonstrates, joint planning is marked by great diversity and what is relevant and works in one area might be quite inappropriate somewhere else. A 'loose-tight' approach may therefore be necessary – *loose* in the sense of encouraging and fostering diversity in service providers and operational management and in attempts at co-ordination, but *tight* in the clear commitment at all levels to creating a climate in which joint planning and service co-ordination are seen as integral to the implementation of a clearly stated and mutually agreed policy in respect of community care.

Wistow and Hardy (1991) conclude a review of joint management schemes by stating that 'effectiveness in community care is to be found no less in the dry detail of management than in the vision of inter-agency collaboration' (p.47). Perhaps the most important message to emerge from the foregoing is the need for modest expectations about what can be achieved in pace and volume through joint planning. In this way, although progress may appear less dramatic, it will amount to genuine progress as distinct from aspirations of intent or ultimately futile exercises in symbolic policy-making. It behoves all of us with a part to play in the policy and practice of community care to ensure that community care planning does not end up as yet another example of symbolic policy making in a policy field that already has more than its fair share of symbols.

6 *No housing – no community care*

Anne Yanetta and Laurie Naumann

Introduction

The major changes in the delivery of community care rely heavily on
the availability of good quality, affordable housing. Whilst health authorities and social work/services departments are undergoing restruc-
turing and change as a result of the community care white papers and
the subsequent legislation, housing providers are themselves facing
upheaval and major change. The most urgent issues facing many
housing agencies are stock transfer and dealing with increasing numbers of homeless people, particularly those under 25 and those whose
mortgage payment is now beyond their means. These urgent demands
on public (or social) rented sector landlords, together with pressure to
secure income and reduce arrears and waiting lists, depress the priority
given to planning and providing accommodation for community care
groups.

This chapter examines the changes taking place in the social rented
sector, discusses the pressures on agencies and looks at the role for
housing providers, staff and committee members, who despite these
pressures, have sought to be innovative and creative.

The UK context

Disappointingly for people working in the housing field, Sir Roy
Griffiths, in his eagerly awaited report *Agenda for Action* (1988) gave
scant recognition of the housing component of community care,
referring to it as the 'bricks and mortar' and making no suggestions

55

about means of ensuring its continued and improved contribution to the delivery of community care services. While change in the management and provision of housing was perhaps not anticipated by him in the same way as for social work and health services, the failure to recognise the completely different funding arrangements for housing and the long-term capital investment complementing the revenue dependent services was regrettable.

Although the White Paper *Caring for People* (1989) covered England, Scotland and Wales, it is remarkable how different the contributions describing the housing involvement were. Token references are made to housing in the English, Scottish and Welsh chapters; these fail to emphasise the strategic contribution made by housing to community care. Only in the Northern Irish White Paper, *People First* (1990), is the housing contribution given greater prominence with eleven paragraphs devoted to housing. An emphasis is placed on the use of mainstream housing by the Northern Ireland Housing Executive (NIHE) and housing associations. It also refers to the importance of enabling conversions and care and repair schemes in the private sector to help older people remain in their own homes. A particular point is made about proposals to harmonise planning cycles between the health and social service boards, NIHE and housing associations, thus preventing problems experienced elsewhere in the UK.

During the 1980s it was clear that, when it came to putting the stated policy into practice, the results varied, not only between the different countries within the United Kingdom, but also quite distinctively at a local level. This is clearly due partly to the absence of proper guidance from the relevant government departments but also to local factors and historical practices. There have been substantial practical problems in involving all the housing agencies in the planning and delivery of services given the differences between the major participants in size, primary objectives and geographical area covered.

The growth of owner occupation, encouraged particularly by the legislation of 1980 that introduced the 'right to buy' (with discount) for secure tenants in the public sector (local authorities, new towns, NIHE and Scottish Special Housing Association (now Scottish Homes)) greatly altered the tenure pattern within the United Kingdom. From 1980 in England and 1986 in Scotland, housing associations also had this right to buy, but in 1989 it was restricted by new assured tenancy legislation. Housing associations, for so long innovators in the provision of housing for care in the community, account for only three per cent of the stock in the UK. This figure will, of course, increase as transfers of stock from local authorities and new towns to housing associations and co-operatives continues, but the dominance of owner-occupation will remain.

The role of housing in community care

'If community care is the body then housing is the backbone' (NFHA, 1989, p.5). Housing clearly has a key role to play in the provision of care in the community. This can be clearly seen in the provision of sheltered housing for elderly people and supported accommodation for people with 'special needs'.

As far back as 1952, the Scottish Housing Advisory Committee recognised that 'special groups are integral parts of the general population and any policy leading to their separation would be undesirable . . . houses for special groups should always be provided as an integral part of normal housing development' (SHAC, 1952, para.16).

It was further recognised that the numbers of houses for 'special groups' should be kept small. This theme was continued in 1988, when the Wagner report stated: 'The emphasis is on the provision of ordinary housing accommodation, with support put into the house as appropriate' (Wagner, 1988, p.16).

The ability of providers in the social rented sector to ensure that the most appropriate housing is available for 'special needs' groups varies and is affected greatly by the funding available and the condition and location of the agencies' stock. There are great variations in the spending patterns.

Funding housing providers

Over the past twelve years, emphasis on government policy has been towards reducing public expenditure. For local authorities, this has led to a massive reduction in Revenue Support Grant (England and Wales) and Housing Support Grant (Scotland), with a greater reliance on rents as the major source of income to pay for management and maintenance costs. This has had an impact on rent levels, creating weekly increases between 1981 and 1989 in Scotland from £5.86 to £16.79 and in England and Wales from £11.39 to £20.64 (Gibb and Munro, 1991).

57

Local authorities have also had to deal with restrictions on their ability to build new houses or carry out major improvement works by the control placed on their level of financial borrowing and, particularly in Scotland, the need to fund building out of capital receipts from the sale of houses to sitting tenants.

Since the passing of the Housing and Housing (Scotland) Acts in 1988, the housing association movement has undergone great change both within and between countries. A detailed account, which space does not permit here, can be found in (Lowe and Hughes, eds., 1992). The former Housing Corporation which covered Great Britain, has been divided into national bodies with responsibility for registering and monitoring housing associations and, additionally in Scotland, with responsibilities as a landlord and the powers to fine private developers and landlords.

The 1988 Acts produced major changes in the rights of tenants, with the introduction to the 'independent rented sector' (housing associations and the private rented market) of assured tenancies and, time limited, short assured (Scotland) or assured shorthold tenancies (England and Wales) for which landlords set their own rents. The legislation also made it easier for landlords to repossess their properties.

These new tenancies came into effect for all new tenants in 1989. Whilst landlords can offer agremeents containing more rights than those given in law (and many housing associations have done so), the legislation provides fewer basic mandatory rights for tenants, by removing them from the fair rent system and excluding them from the right to buy which local authority, new town, Scottish Homes (ex-SSHA) and NIHE tenants retain.

When the new tenancies were introduced, the funding of housing associations also changed, with the requirement now to fund the loan element of the development costs with private finance rather than the Housing Association Grant, which is being gradually reduced.

Revenue funding in community care projects has, in the main, relied on housing benefit or DSS residential care allowances, with revenue 'gaps' met by social work supplementation or top-up funding, as well as contributions from relatives, charities or health authority bridging finance. The dowry system, used by many health authorities in England and Wales, has provided an incentive in the hospital closure pro-gramme and a degree of security to some supported housing projects. This funding facility has rarely been used in Scotland, where there continues to be a heavier reliance on residential or hospital care.

Each financial change has created difficulties for all housing agencies including those providing accommodation for community care projects. For residents and tenants, meeting the cost of supported housing or residential homes has generally been possible through the welfare benefit system; however, those people who have capital above the maximum allowed levels, or who gain employment thereby losing some or all of their housing benefit entitlement, continue to face problems.

With the implementation of the NHS and Community Care Act 1990, major changes occur from April 1993 in the funding of care in the community. Money will be transferred from the DSS eventually reaching the local social work/service authority, which will then pay for the support and care services required where the costs cannot be met by the resident or tenant through either their own income or housing benefit paid separately by the housing authority. These services can be provided by the local authority or bought in from voluntary organisations, housing associations or the private sector. However, if the money is not 'ring-fenced' community care funding will face the same pressures as all other local authority services.

Type of community care housing

There has been a remarkable change of attitude among the main public sector housing providers towards providing housing for community care. The housing association movement in its present form has grown from almost nothing in the early seventies to become a major contributor of a range of housing resources for community care, perhaps most noticeably in the field of sheltered housing, but also in a variety of hostels and supported accommodation with different degrees of staffing complements. These have ranged from some quite large, fairly traditional institutional-type developments to the widespread use of mainstream housing of various forms including core and cluster, dispersed hostels, group homes and cluster flats, many of which have now been widely adopted by local authorities, new towns and other public sector providers.

Since the 1970s, advances have been made in the development and provision of housing for elderly people. Sheltered housing, with resident warden support has developed to provide 'very-sheltered' or 'care housing' for more frail elderly people at one end of the scale and, at the other, amenity housing and care and repair projects.

The use of 'general needs' or 'mainstream' housing provides one of

59

the most effective means of integrating community care projects into a neighbourhood, avoiding one of the accusations made towards sheltered housing or large hostels of 'being different' or easily identifiable as housing for certain groups of people.

Core and cluster models, or dispersed hostels, allow residents to live in a domestic environment with support provided as required. Planning permission, with the need for fire escapes, fire doors, etc. that would make any house 'look different', is not normally required for houses with fewer than six residents. The support provided can also be very flexible and move between premises thus avoiding the need for the upheaval associated with tenants having to move to find or receive support.

Many questions are raised about the necessity and appropriateness of registering all supported housing and community care projects with the social services/work authority under the relevant legislation. While it is the responsibility of the local authority to decide upon registration, it needs to be borne in mind that it does have implications for tenants who could lose some of their basic right to security if care and support rather than accommodation becomes the key factor. Clearly registration authorities are becoming increasingly flexible as greater emphasis is placed upon dispersed provision and use is made of new technology to maintain contact, but the conflict of interest can still occur.

Timescales in planning housing for community care

Local authorities are required to produce housing plans in Scotland or housing investment programmes in England, detailing the projected need for housing in their locality and making a bid for funding and loan consent. Housing associations and co-operatives have been required since 1989 to publish three year business plans, which are used in the assessment of bids for funding from the four national housing bodies.

Given the timescale required for any new building project, it is vital that the consultation for planning community care housing is done at both local and strategic levels. The planning process for care in the community has developed unevenly in the UK, not least between Scotland and England.

Unlike England and Wales, joint planning is not a statutory requirement in Scotland and consequently different regions have responded in very different ways. Research by Kohls (1989) showed that little progress in the collaborative planning process has been made since the publication of the Scottish Office circular in 1985. Kohls further states that 'substantial and comprehensive changes and development in the pattern and level of services for the Scottish Health Authorities priority groups have not taken place and are unlikely to do so unless more commitment to the implementation of joint plans is shown by the Scottish Office' (Kohls, 1989, p.33). The evidence in February 1992 in Glasgow was that no housing association or co-op had been consulted at all in the preparation of the local community care plan (CCPs).

The White Paper *Caring for People* stated as the first of its six key objectives on service delivery the need 'to promote the development of domiciliary, day and respite services to enable people to live in their own homes whenever feasible and sensible' (para. 1.11).

Ministers in England and Wales initially rejected amendments to the legislation that would have required social service authorities to consult with housing authorities in their areas during the preparation of their CCPs. Interestingly, the Scottish Office accepted the principle of an amendment of a similar kind at the first attempt; and the Department of Health and the Welsh Office only conceded at a later stage.

The NHS and Community Care Act (Ss 46 and 52) now places a requirement on both social work/social service departments and health authorities in England, Wales and Scotland to produce community care plans from April 1992.

Housing authorities must therefore be consulted by social work and health authorities before their community care plans are published. What is not prescribed, however, is the scope and level of this consultation and there is evidence of uneven levels of partnerships. While half the Scottish CCPs are joint between the social work authorities and health boards, only one is joint with the six relevant statutory housing agencies.

Comprehensive planning for care in the community also requires adequate data on numbers of people in need of services and sharing of data from various departments. In Scotland, work has only now (1992) started on the development of a common information base for health, social work, housing and voluntary sector interests.

Conclusion

The new care in the community proposals require a fresh approach by all concerned, who must become better at listening to the consumers of the service and better at understanding the range of skills and pressures associated with the social work and health professions. The housing achievements in the past have often been due to particular local pressures or even individual enthusiasm. The consequence has been that the most significant contributions in the housing field have been made through negotiations between individuals in local and health authorities' housing agencies or voluntary organisations.

For any major shift from hospital to community, it is necessary that the retrained staff, day centres and support facilities are in place to prevent the problems of the 1980s when discharged mentally ill patients were placed in the community and became the responsibility of the local homeless persons' officer. These same facilities will also be of major assistance to those currently in the community, being cared for or supported by families, partners or friends, many without the help of respite care.

Care in the community needs to be adequately financed. It has long been recognised that care and support in small domestic or ordinary settings is often more, and not less, expensive than large scale institutionalized care.

Improvement to the housing service has happened at the same time as it faces increasing pressures of financial control, problems of the systems-built houses of the 1950s and 1960s, the move to transfer stock from the public sector and the increase in those accepted as homeless, who, in 1990, stood at 169,526 in Great Britain – a 221 per cent increase since 1980 (Greve, 1990).

Despite these problems, there have been success stories. Local authority housing departments have provided housing for projects run by social work departments, voluntary organisations and health boards, and the private sector is an important contributor in the residential field.

The opportunities for full care in the community should not however depend simply on location, nor on a local self-help group campaigning for services. Rather it requires a proper lead from all the government departments and a commitment at both national and local government level to provide effective and comprehensive care to all those who require it.

In 1975, the Scottish Development Department published the Morris committee report on 'Housing and Social Work – a joint approach' that stated in its summary:

> 'The development of effective co-operation [between housing and social work] will not be possible unless both services
> (a) understand each other's capacity, policies and management
> (b) understand the demarcation of their respective responsibilities
> (c) establish and maintain good communications . . .
> (d) are aware of constraints on resources' (Morris Report, p.5)

Eighteen years on, the recommendation remains true. Housing officers need to understand the new tasks required of social workers, and the demands placed on them by the legislation. Social workers need to understand the planning and development time required to provide or obtain appropriate housing, the increasing demands made by growing waiting lists and the range of allocation policies in operation.

As well as developing trust and understanding between the agencies and professions, it must be recognised that housing is provided as a general community service whereas community care, at its most important, is personally designed to meet the need of an individual. Much can be learnt from working together and understanding each other's roles. This trust and co-operation work would be considerably enhanced with the practical assistance of common planning cycles.

There is now an even clearer shared objective of working together to ensure ordinary housing in ordinary streets as the basis of providing care and support in the community. Without such housing there cannot be effective care in the community.

7 Coming together in diversity: voluntary organizations and community care planning *Averil Osborn*

Introduction

The voluntary sector contains a diversity of interests with various parts to play in community care and its planning. Assumptions to the contrary, that organizations within the voluntary sector are all the same, could lead to inappropriate expectations. To become involved in community care planning, voluntary groups and those in the statutory sector need to understand the parts voluntary groups are able to play, for example as service providers, consumer groups, campaigning or policy bodies. Participation introduces new tasks and skills. This will challenge voluntary bodies and those in the statutory sector alike.

A diverse collection

Within the voluntary sector are a large number of organizations with an interest in the community care of adults. Some, such as Councils of Voluntary Service, have a broad-based interest whilst others exist for a specific group of people such as those with dementia or learning difficulties. Their activities and purposes vary, from the agency directly providing community care services, to user and carer groups, policy and campaigning bodies, advice agencies, and independent advocacy services. This list is not exhaustive. Size and resources also vary from small unfunded groups to large providers with an extensive staff and considerable annual turnover. Geographical coverage ranges from across Scotland or the UK wide to very local. Philosophies vary from the radical groups who reject collaboration with the statutory sector to traditional bodies who sit comfortably with the public sector and its bureaucracy.

The shift towards the new world of community care has created increased expectations of 'the voluntary sector'. These focus upon contracting to provide services on behalf of the statutory sector and on adding the consumer voice to planning debates. However, these expectations do not always fit the real and diverse nature and capacities within the voluntary sector. Voluntary groups are not necessarily 'close to the people' and able to speak with the consumer voice, nor are they all equally able and willing to contract with the statutory sector to provide services. Many groups with key concerns about community care services or consumers are neither of these, many do one or the other. It is unhelpful to treat the voluntary sector as an homogeneous grouping.

Voluntary groups and community care in the past

Voluntary organizations have undertaken a wide range of activities in the past, resourced through their own means or through statutory sector grants or project money. A minority provided services as agents of the statutory sector. Relationships with the statutory sector were not generally dictated within a comprehensive framework of service planning but arose in *ad hoc* ways over the years. Indeed, until the advent of the NHS and Community Care Act, voluntary organization involvement in authority-wide planning of services had been patchy. Joint planning, involving the local authorities and the health authorities, permitted their involvement, but had developed variably. Also, experience of trying to play an effective part was subsumed within the limited effectiveness of joint planning as a whole.

Anticipated involvement of the voluntary sector

The 1990s are seeing the introduction of community care planning, an increased use made of the voluntary sector to deliver community care services under contract, and attempts to involve consumers in shaping their services. Voluntary groups therefore have much more scope to become involved in planning. However, these opportunities come at a challenging time for many voluntary organizations regarding their own future, security and role. The scene is changing with the growth of service contracts, a diminution of grant aid for other functions, pressures on charitable giving and an increased interest in carer and user groups. There are fears that smaller groups will perish whilst more sophisticated, larger ones will monopolize the contracts. Voluntary sector development agencies best placed to facilitate participation are themselves vulnerable as statutory sector funders tend to undervalue bodies able to inform, train, develop and support the service providers and user or carer groups.

Community care plans were published for the first time in April 1992. Plans are expected to be needs led and are intended to share a more appropriate range and choice of flexible services. The voluntary sector must be consulted in the preparation of the plans. As defined in the NHS and Community Care Act 1990 (para.46) the local authority must consult:

> 'Such voluntary organisations as appear to the authority to represent the interests of persons who use or are likely to use any of the community care services within the area of the authority or the interests of private carers who, within that area, provide care to persons for whom, in the exercise of their social services functions, the local authority have a power or a duty to provide a service.
>
> Such voluntary housing agencies and other bodies as appear to the local authority to provide housing or community care services in their area'.

The subsequent guidance, issued separately for England, Wales and Scotland, also includes black and ethnic minority communities, umbrella voluntary organizations and voluntary organizations concerned with the interests of volunteers (DOH, 1990; SED/SHHD, 1991; Welsh Office, 1990). Voluntary organizations will be invited into planning primarily as the voice of consumers (users or carers) or as service providers.

The imperative to stimulate a 'mixed economy of care' is also built into community care planning; local authorities, in particular, must plan to increase the purchase of services from commercial and voluntary organizations whilst reducing the proportion of services directly supplied and managed by themselves. Voluntary organizations will become increasingly important suppliers, working under contract to social services or social work departments or the health service. The private sector will have an increased role but this is not the subject of this chapter.

Other potential roles for voluntary organizations

The development of user sensitive services shaped by needs-led planning requires more of voluntary organizations than the provision of community care services under contract and the representation of user and carer groups' views. Other contributions are important but currently less sought after.

Advocacy services

Community care in the future is intended to offer users and carers choice and be responsive to the user and carer voices. The most vulnerable may need assistance to find their voice or to exercise choice. Involvement in formal community care planning, in the individual assessment of needs or in making a complaint may require support from an independent advocacy service. All these activities are intended to inform community care planning, the first directly and the others through the feeding up of information from complaints and assessments.

Local information services for the public

Good, easily obtainable information is needed about local community care services. Without information it is more difficult for users and carers to make choices or become involved.

Complementary care services and activities

The statutory sector will never be the sole source of care in the community. There will always be a need for complementary services and cognizance must be taken of these by planners. Voluntary organizations pursue innovation and offer services or activities not seen by the statutory sector as priorities. Some of this will be grant aided and some funded independently.

Service support and development

Voluntary sector development agencies can catalyse development and support the providers of community care services. This may be particularly important to smaller community groups or rapidly expanding providers. Help with information, training, service development, good management, fundraising and so forth are given.

Support to carers and users groups

Some voluntary agencies are well placed to develop user and carer groups who can then decide their own role in planning.

Policy, research and campaigning

Some voluntary groups undertake high quality policy and research of relevance to community care issues and campaign to influence plans based on sound evidence and argument.

The functions described above reflect the diversity within the voluntary sector. All have their place in the develpment of care in the community and therefore in the planning of this care.

Formal community care planning

To participate appropriately in the formal community care planning processes, voluntary groups need to

- take stock of their own interest and role(s) in community care and hence their likely involvement in community care planning
- organize for effective involvement
- consider wider obligations to involve marginalized voluntary groups, user and carers, or community interests.

This is described in the recent Nuffield Institute/Age Concern Scotland pack (Osborn, 1991).

Taking stock

Taking stock enables a group to consider its aims, what it does or intends doing and with what priority, and for whom it can act or speak. It clarifies whether the group sees itself as a contracted supplier of services, a consumer group or in some other capacity. This provides a basis for deciding whether engagement in community care planning is a relevant activity for the group.

Confirmation that community care is its concern is the
'Community care' is jargon to some who may not identify their interesᴛ
as falling within it. Volunteers providing lunches for frail elderly people
in a rural church hall may not recognize their role in the larger scheme
of things, nor recognize that the larger scheme could significantly
influence the wellbeing of 'their' older people and the service the group
provides. Such recognition is a prerequisite to deliberate participation
in community care planning.

Groups of organized users or carers may be expected to voice directly
the views and experience of users and carers in community care
planning debates, whether or not this is one of their objectives and
priorities. Within this, the voices of users and carers need to be
differentiated as they are not identical. Other voluntary groups, even
if some of their members happen to be users or carers, will not
automatically have this voice. Legitimacy to speak as users or carers is
emerging as a major issue. The assumption that 'voluntary sector'
means the consumer voice is decreasing, but is still an area of
confusion, exacerbated by scarcity of user and carer groups able to take
this on and, if necessary, to challenge others claiming to speak for
them. Groups in close touch with users or carers can speak knowledge-
ably about them based on valuable experience and have important
things to say but only groups of users or carers speak as carers or users.

Any group speaking for people or organizations with a stake in
community care has to address its accountability to those for whom
it speaks. How does it consult, involve and report back to this
constituency? What is the nature of its accountability to others in
authority, such as the management committee, the parent body or an
external funder?

Organizing for effective involvement

As the local authority takes the lead in community care planning, the
discussion here concentrates on local authority structures. Where a
joint (single) plan is not produced with the health authorities (District
Health Authorities and Family Health Service Authorities or Health
Boards) then voluntary organizations may need to look at separate
participation in the health authority planning process and also see what
the planning agreement entails.

Statutory organizations will prefer to deal with fewer organizations,
rather than contemplate a continuing direct involvement with a myriad

of groups. A local authority can have hundreds of groups within its area, although it may only hold information on those it funds.

Seats on formal planning groups are limited and it is practical for voluntary groups to band together to become involved in formal community care planning, often as a forum, e.g. the North Yorkshire Forum, the Grampian Voluntary Organizations Forum. An authority-wide forum enables an overview across the whole local authority area and 'care groups'.

There is no blueprint as to how community care planning should be organized, but it is likely that planning will then be broken down by geographical area and 'care group'. Voluntary groups are likely to organize to reflect the local authority planning structures, for example forming district groups or groups with specific care/client group interest. This makes it easier to shadow formal planning and to seek direct representation. Voluntary groups whose interests do not slot neatly into the chosen geography or care groupings will have to fit in as best they can. It seems unlikely that official structures will adjust to accommodate the variability and lack of formality within the voluntary sector. Some fear resultant bureaucratization within the voluntary sector, if it should respond by modelling its operation along similar lines to the statutory sector.

Organization for participation in planning requires considerable resourcing, which is usually not available. Groups must be recruited to the forum, briefed and continually updated and consulted on community care matters. This requires administration, information and training inputs. Representatives must be selected and supported.

In particular, representatives need the following:

- an understanding of community care issues and the planning system and process
- an appreciation of the aims and membership of the forum they represent, and channels of accountability and consultation within that body
- an understanding of codes of practice, manifestos or charters to be upheld
- an appreciation of the tasks expected as a representative and the time commitment involved; a job description helps
- administrative and other practical backup to help with things such as the setting up meetings and circulating of papers.

Joint planning experience indicates that bridging the gap between the statutory sector officials and voluntary groups can be stressful, requiring the representative to understand both worlds without fully belonging to either.

Representation is never ideal. If representatives raise awkward issues their bona fides to represent may well be challenged. Every effort will be needed to define the constituency and to involve the constituents so that representation has a firm base.

Voluntary organizations may not always agree. There may be an uneasy balance between making common cause based on shared values and the pressure to compete in the marketplace, for example as rival providers seeking contracts or grants, or as rival campaigners championing different care groups. Speaking for a grouping of diverse autonomous bodies, it may be important to present a range of views rather than the dilute consensus. This dilemma is lessened where the number of representatives is greater, as they can then present a range of views.

Individuals in the statutory sector with responsibilities for preparing plans may not regard consultation as a high priority for their time and resources. A common complaint from voluntary groups is that they are consulted too late and without any real commitment from the statutory authority to respond.

Wider responsibilities

Powerful, professionalized and skilful groups will probably negotiate their involvement in community care planning, either directly or through some forum. There are fears that others will be left outside. Collective action could moderate this, but a 'forum' may itself become a barrier if access is not open and its procedures not tailored for the less formal, less bureaucratized groups. Current failures to involve black and minority ethnic groups, small community based groups and the generally underdeveloped nature of user and carer involvement present major concerns. Involvement issues are well documented in the evaluation of the All Wales Strategy (McGrath, 1990; Welsh Office, 1991). Arguments for involvement and the fundamental importance of good accessible information are well put by the Welsh Consumer Council (1990).

Voluntary groups could extend participation in community care planning both by ensuring that other groups are drawn in and by involving those within their own network more. Groups can educate their own members and service users on community care matters,

71

consult them more and assist in setting up and supporting independent groups who speak for themselves, such as user groups in the day centres they run or consumer groups in a local community.

Challenges to voluntary organizations

Involvement in community care planning poses many challenges to voluntary organizations. They will need to become clear as to why they seek involvement. The increasing exposure of their diversity runs parallel to the necessity for closer collaboration than hitherto in order to gain an input. At a period of great change and pressure, they need to find time, resources and new skills to be effective in this new arena. There are also challenges in opening up planning to those whose voices are weak – smaller groups, users and carers, minority communities. Effective involvement is more problematic where the health and local authorities are not planning well together and where housing remains on the periphery.

Challenge to the statutory sector

The challenges to those in the health service and local authorities are no less. They are expected to change from traditional service-led planning to needs-led and consumer conscious planning, to split their purchasing and providing functions, to develop care management and to create community care plans all within a very short space of time. Involving voluntary and consumer groups takes their time and needs their resources. Involvement raises conflicts about the place and primacy of professional judgment, questions existing power and the need to empower others, opens up planning and exposes gaps and inadequate provision. It means resisting the convenient behind the scenes deals that bypass formal planning. It requires an ability to work with a much wider range of groups and individuals who are not always versed in committee procedure, who do not share the jargon, who may be angry or uncertain, who want their agenda to be addressed and who will certainly want to see action.

Whatever the outcomes, the NHS and Community Care Act has placed community care on political agendas and brought it forward as a major area for the health and local authorities. It has increased attention to community care planning and has both drawn attention to voluntary groups and forced questions about their future direction and functions. It has brought users and carers into the frame. The impact and effect of this is at this stage enlightened speculation.

8 The role of the independent sector in community care planning Bob Bessell

The mushroom growth of the private homes

The obvious starting point for a discussion of the role of the independent sector in community care planning is the mushroom growth in the number of private old people's homes since 1979, when there were about 10,000 places, to the present figure, which is well in excess of 100,000 excluding the registered nursing homes, so that the private sector is now significantly bigger than the public and voluntary sectors combined.

The demography

This highly artificial development, based in part on a quirk of social policy, compounded by business opportunism, is also a reflection of an increase in the number of older people in the population, which has been a characteristic of the demography of Britain and all the western nations throughout the twentieth century, so that between 1861 and 1978, the life expectancy of a woman, at birth, has risen from 43 to 76.1 years, an increase of 77 per cent. In 1951, there were 5.5 million people in the United Kingdom over the age of 65 years, while by 1981 the figure had risen to 9.1 million, an increase of 65 per cent.

However, in the last two decades of the twentieth century, the total number of people over the age of 65 years has more or less stabilized, but there is currently a dramatic increase in the very oldest section of the population, so that over the next twenty years the total number of people over the age of 85 years will increase from 0.9 million to 1.35 million, an increase of 50 per cent.

The assets of elderly people

Another factor that has tended to boost the private sector is the increase in the value of the assets owned by elderly people, particularly the state retirement pension. First introduced on a means-tested basis in 1908 for everyone over the age of 70 years, it has been available to all women over 60 years and men over 65 since 1940. Additionally there are welfare benefits, such as the age-related social security payments, that are exclusively for older people and others, such as Attendance Allowance, for which older people are the principal qualifiers.

Occupational pensions are still much more prevalent with younger, older people, but the proportion is changing year by year, as is the ownership of housing, so that although 58 per cent of all retired people now own their own house, without mortgage, the distribution is skewed in favour of younger, retired people. However, the overall percentage is increasing at roughly one per cent a year and will continue until it matches the general population of 70 per cent home ownership.

The domination of issues concerning old people

The combination of the massive increase in the number of elderly people, the material resources they have accumulated and the unintended consequences of the benefit changes in social security payments means that considerations relating to elderly people totally dominate social policy in community care planning.

Of course one has to have regard to the needs of people with learning difficulties, people who are disabled by mental illness and younger, physically disabled people, but even their combined totals are dwarfed by the issues relating to older, disabled people and, in particular, by the growth in the number of private old people's homes.

It is, however, a moot point whether all of these private homes can properly be described as independent, as approximately half of the places are paid for by the Department of Social Security from public funds.

Social security support for private residential care

The story of how this came about is quite extraordinary and illustrates not only the difficulties of definition but also the far-reaching consequences of failing to think through changes in benefit regulations.

75

In the period before 1979, when the Conservative Party was in opposition, they received a number of complaints that the benefit regulations of the time were unduly restrictive and, in particular, that elderly people without means could only be admitted to local authority homes for which, at the time there were long waiting-lists, whereas accommodation was available at no greater cost in privately-owned homes.

Accordingly, when the Conservatives came to power in 1979, they changed the rules to enable elderly people without means to claim social security payments for private homes. This was seen at the time as a minor administrative change to abolish an unnecessary restriction and thereby add the facilities of the private sector to the over-stretched local authorities.

The actual effect was rather different, best illustrated by the fact that in 1979, the cost of public payments to the private Homes was a modest £10 million, whereas in 1991 it is estimated that the cost was in excess of £1,600 million, which even allowing for inflation almost certainly makes it the most expensive change ever undertaken in social welfare.

The consequence has been a major distortion of social welfare provision, because the social security payments are only available for residential care, without any assessment of need (with regard to independent sector placements). The Audit Commission described this as 'the perverse incentive' (1986) as none of the social security money can be used for services such as home care or adaptations to people's own homes.

In view of the distortion that has occurred because the total amount of money now paid out is both so great and restricted to residential care, it is not possible to know what the optimum pattern would be if the same amount of money could be spent on a wider range of provision. However, the present position is that approximately half of the places in private old people's homes are paid for mainly from social security payments and to that extent one questions whether they can accurately be described as 'independent'.

Ever since the escalation in costs of the social security payments for private residential care became apparent, it has been obvious that some change will have to be made, but there is no easy answer and politicians have repeatedly drawn back from grasping the nettle. The costs and the distorting effects have grown at an increasing rate so that the whole debate on community care, not only in the independent sector, is now dominated by this issue.

In 1986, the Secretary of State for Health and Social Services, Norman Fowler, asked Sir Roy Griffiths to report on the issue. The Griffiths Report, *Community Care: Agenda for Action* (1988) came to two principal conclusions: that doing nothing was not an option and that the only viable course of action was to transfer the bulk of the social security money being spent on residential care to the local authority Social Services Departments but give them the freedom to spend the money on any form of care rather than restrict it to residential care.

After prolonged debate, these proposals were adopted in a Government White Paper and eventually passed into law in the National Health Service and Community Care Act, 1990.

The original timetable for implementation of the major change was April 1991, which was then deferred until April 1993, conveniently after the General Election. Meanwhile, the amounts of money involved have grown alarmingly and a whole industry of private residential care has been built on the flawed foundation of what was perceived as a minor administrative change, which has had unsupportable consequences.

In a feeble endeavour to limit the exponential increase in costs, in 1986 the Department of Health and Social Security imposed limits on the amount of money that could be claimed by an individual and subsequently increased these amounts arbitrarily year by year by amounts less than the actual increase in costs claimed by the homes. The result was a severe cash squeeze, which was first of all resolved by some home owners claiming the element of personal allowances of residents, thereby frequently leaving them penniless, but when even this was insufficient to meet what the home owners claimed was the shortfall between income and expenditure, then either relatives were pressed to contribute or the amenities of residents dependent upon social security were reduced.

The difficulties were exacerbated by the effect of the Residential Homes Act, 1984, which effectively insisted upon raising standards and therefore costs in independent and voluntary homes.

The problem became so acute in 1990 that, acting on a very suspect research report prepared by Price Waterhouse, the Secretary of State for Social Security made a one-off substantial increase in the residential care allowances in nursing homes, which has been repeated, although to a less degree, in 1991 in respect of residential care homes.

The effect of these two special increases alone has been to increase the expected cost to the Treasury in 1991 from £1,000 million to £1,650

77

million and all for the sake of postponing an embarrassing issue until after the election.

To compound the mischief, the local authorities wrestling with what they perceived as a continuing shortage of funds also saw the social security funds as a supplementary source of income for their own residential care. Advised by private consultants, for very large fees, from about 1990 onwards they set up a variety of organizations all of which had the sole aim of attracting government social security funds for the support of residents who would otherwise be the financial responsibility of the local authority.

The Government's first response to this strategem has been to define existing residents of transferred homes as the continuing responsibility of the local authority, but that still leaves the loophole of future residents and as the turnover rate of residents in residential care is at least one-third each year, this still makes the exercise very attractive to the local authorities.

In view of the sorry history of this saga, it is equally obvious that the change when it comes will be much more disruptive than it need have been if the nettle had been grasped when the problem was analysed five years ago and the principal sufferers will be the frail elderly people who will be caught in the political cross-fire.

Transition day

The scenario in April 1993, when the Government finally plucked up courage to implement the transfer of decision-making in individual cases to the local authorities, was as unfortunate as it was predictable, and the danger is that the resulting uproar is so great that it will obscure the inevitability of what had to be done.

Unfortunately, the sheer size of the private residential sector, which has been so recently but so massively inflated, meant that it could not be sustained, particularly now the local authorities are free to spend the funds on alternative forms of care.

As a result, many residential homes face insolvency and it is hardly surprising that their owners are making the maximum protest and, in particular, the most of the hardships faced by their residents. Local authorities are being besieged for money from all sources and, as a result, are under maximum pressure just when they are putting a whole range of new assessment and allocation procedures into operation.

It is only when these earthquakes have subsided that it will be possible to get on with developing a truly independent sector of community care and to consider the fundamental question of the extent to which frail elderly people should be expected to utilize the assets they have accumulated during their lives, in place of receiving assistance from the public purse, which effectively enhances the legacy they can leave to their heirs.

It is not possible to construct a 'pure' resolution to this problem based on the principles that either disabled people should first of all have to utilise all of their own resources before receiving welfare benefits from the public purse or their private assets should be entirely disregarded.

In the first place, it is simply not possible to disentangle public and private wealth. Almost all privately-owned houses have been bought with the assistance of income-tax relief on mortgage payments and there have been similar income-tax allowances for private pensions. Moreover, the core income of almost all elderly people is the state retirement pension and it is an entirely moot point as to whether this is public money paid out of taxation receipts or merely a deferred repayment of contributions to the central exchequer paid in throughout the working life.

As if this were not enough, the position is further complicated by the VAT regulations so that, unlike other EEC countries, no VAT is payable on house building, although paradoxically, it is payable on extensions and adaptations, and the VAT position with regard to domestic care agencies seems to vary according to the opinions of the local VAT inspector, whereas residential care homes and nursing homes are exempt from VAT.

The question then arises, is the whole subject such a tangled web that it is not possible to resolve it on the basis of principle, with the consequence that social policy will be determined either by accident or whoever shouts loudest.

This is a fair description of the present state of affairs, but it does not have to be the case, and one of the few reassuring features is that it is the lack of forethought that is the cause of the present arrangements breaking down and gives the impetus for change.

An alternative approach

An alternative approach is to examine the needs of elderly disabled people and, in particular, to consider their wishes and then to see how the services needed could best be organized without preconceptions about the public, private and voluntary sectors, but always starting from where we are now.

This may seem impossibly utopian but there are two major indicators of the value of this approach. The first is that according to the General Household Survey, over 91 per cent of all retired people live and die in their own homes, without any services or assistance from public funds apart from the state retirement pension and marginally increased attention for their GP, but less than the allowance GPs receive for their elderly patients. This would seem to indicate that consulting people's wishes is not likely to prove unduly expensive, particularly as there are also very strong indications that large sums of public money could be put to much better use.

For instance, most orthopaedic wards in hospitals have a high percentage of beds occupied by elderly patients who require no clinical services, but who cannot return home because there are not the domiciliary services to care for them and this example could be multiplied many times. As the average cost of a bed in an orthopaedic ward is at least £1,000 a week, the resolution of this anomaly would release significant funds either to improve the standard of health care or else to pay for improved domiciliary services.

We have, therefore, a situation in which more than nine out of ten people live and die in their own homes, without significant extra help, so that the problems largely revolve around the remaining eight and a half per cent of the elderly population and even if more domiciliary services are required, then at least some of this money could come from resolving anomalies such as the misplaced patients in the orthopaedic wards.

The bigger issue is whether all of the people currently being admitted to residential care homes and nursing homes need to be there and, more particularly, whether there would be any saving if they received substantially more domiciliary care in their own homes.

So far there is no conclusive research evidence on this subject and the picture is obscured by the self-interest of the public service unions on the one hand and the private home-owners on the other.

Provided the Government of the day sticks to the timetable of the NHS and Community Care Act and does transfer the bulk of the social security funds to the local authorities in April 1993, then this subject should be resolved, as not only will the care managers have the freedom to allocate funds to whichever service seems most cost effective, but they will also have the incentive of limited funds to encourage them to take their task seriously.

The need for even-handedness

This will still leave anomalies like VAT to be resolved, but this is a small matter compared with the present imbalance in favour of residential care. However, a more serious course of concern is the difficulty of care managers in maintaining even-handedness between the private sector on the one hand and the facilities provided directly by the local authorities, which will be competing for the same funds, on the other. The solution would be for the local authorities to reduce significantly the volume of services they provide directly and to concentrate instead on the regulation and inspection of private and voluntary sector provision.

Because they have a responsibility of last resort, the local authorities would need to preserve a skeleton service both of residential and domiciliary care, and there is some evidence that the public sector is at the forefront of innovation, but there is certainly no evidence of efficiency in providing a mass public service. The major problem in raising residential standards lies in the poor standard of much local authority provision and the public service unions are a byword in introducing restrictive practices into the Home Help Service, with rules such as forbidding their members to clean above five feet from the floor or to engage in tasks not specifically included in their job descriptions, when versatility and adaptability are the essence of the service.

The picture then seems to be emerging of a range of services based on the vast majority of people remaining in their own homes and with more of an emphasis on domiciliary care largely provided by private organizations, but where this is uneconomical or otherwise inappropriate, then a move to residential care would be indicated. Most of this would also be provided in the private sector, but with the local authority preserving a strategic reserve both of domiciliary and residential services.

On this basis, the exact boundaries between domiciliary and residential care will be determined in the light of events and may well change over the years.

On reflection, this also seems to be a fair basis for the evolution of services for other groups of disabled people who should benefit from

81

the attention currently being given to the needs of elderly disabled people.

However, all of this will only work if some of the artificial barriers between welfare and housing are demolished. Fortunately there are signs that the importance of improved mobility in all types of housing is being appreciated, but there is still a problem about the traditional divide between the housing and welfare, with the former concentrating solely on fit people and accepting little responsibility for those who are frail. Until this division is excised, it will not be possible to formulate a coherent and unified social policy.

9 *Planning for community mental health care* *Judy Renshaw*

This chapter considers the ways in which provision is made at present for adults with mental health problems, the tasks and challenges posed, the requirements of the new community care policy and the outcome of experience in this field so far. Elderly people with dementia require a rather different service response and merit separate consideration.

Needs and resources

The bulk of mental health resources are found in hospitals and serve the needs of in-patients, while most people with mental health problems who require care are in the community at any one time. Although the balance of resources has shifted to some extent over the last decade, this pattern remains remarkably unchanged. The Mental Health Foundation (1990) has pointed out the gross anomaly of over £2,000 million expenditure in the NHS, mainly on 60,000 in-patients, while less than half of this sum was spent on benefits and local authority care for 5.9 million people with mental health problems in the community.

Mental health, like all community care groups, suffers from a fragmentation of responsibility between different agencies, perverse incentives to provide residential rather than domiciliary care, a mismatch of resources to meet the requirements of policies and the need for bridging finance, and inadequate training for community care.

Mental health has additional problems since the new Act and associated policy guidance have been unable to give local authorities as clear a lead as they have for other groups. The boundaries between health and social care are arguably more blurred and the involvement of health professionals in decisions concerning individuals is undoubtedly stronger. Additionally, the prevention of mental ill-health spreads far beyond professional mental health care or crisis counselling to housing, employment, education and child care.

Tasks and challenges

The balance of resources has to shift towards the community in order to match the needs. The balance also has to shift towards *social care*, which is frequently the most valued and helpful aspect of services. People can gain little from therapy and treatment if they have nowhere satisfactory to live, are inadequately fed and clothed or have nowhere to go during the day and no social contacts. Services have traditionally emphasised 'medical' needs and failed to help with the basics of life.

The views of service users need to be listened to more often and more carefully. Individual users frequently know what is helpful to them, a fact that tends to be forgotten by many treatment regimes that make major decisions about people's lives.

New community services need to be very clear about whom they are to serve and tailor their activities accordingly. Many of the community mental health centres (CMHCs) that developed during the 1980s served mainly people whose needs were short term, who responded well to counselling and behaviour therapy (RDP, 1989). These people's problems are arguably 'less severe'. Awareness of this phenomenon has led planners to focus the work of some of the newer CMHCs more carefully, in order to meet the needs of people in the community who have long-term problems. Targeting this group is not easy, however, and there are managerial and professional obstacles to overcome (Patmore and Weaver, 1991).

Resettlement of people from long-stay hospitals is a major concern in many authorities. Their needs differ from those already living in the community, partly due to their lives in hospital and partly their age and abilities. Authorities will have to develop a range of supported accommodation and other services, such as training in daily living, to enable them to live in ordinary settings.

The problem of homelessness has been particularly visible in recent years in all of the large cities in Britain. As many as 40 per cent of the homeless population appear to suffer from significant mental health problems (Walid and McCarthy, 1989; Weller et al. 1987). While some would suggest that the answer is a return to the institutions, others have pointed out that this suggestion 'is equivalent to suggesting that workhouses should be re-established to end unemployment' (Whitehead, 1991). The prevalence of mental illness has always been high among homeless people and the present situation is as much a consequence of housing policy as it is of mental health policy. A proper solution will require a co-ordinated approach from both sides.

The number of people in prison who have mental health problems has also received attention of late. A similar cry of 'return to the hospitals' can be seen to be misleading if the characteristics of the populations in both settings are examined. One study indicates that the *proportion* of people with mental health problems in prison has remained steady although the total number has risen (Renshaw, 1990). A problem remains for people who commit minor criminal offences and who fail to receive the psychiatric help they need. Collaboration between the criminal justice system and mental health agencies is essential if a better solution for this group is to be found.

The new policy

The new community care policy will not be able to address all of the tasks ahead or solve all of these problems. It does not attempt to alter the disparity between hospital and community health services. It will, however, make a small shift in the balance of resources between agencies and has set down requirements for the co-ordination of care for people discharged from hospital.

National mental health policy is still based on the 1975 White Paper *Better Services for the Mentally Ill* and its update in the 1985 response to the Social Services Committee.

The mental illness specific grant

The extra emphasis given to local authorities may help to bolster the position of social care. Some new resources have already come their way from April 1991, in the form of the Mental Illness Specific Grant (MISG). The grant is allocated to each authority (on a formula basis) for social care, in agreement with local health authorities, for either adult mental health or dementia services. The inclusion of people with dementia was a point of some debate and many commentators feel that this group should have been the subject of a separate initiative, especially in view of the rather small overall size of the grant. Some concern was also expressed about the requirement for health authorities to agree to the plans, in case the new services might have an excessively medical orientation.

The grant in 1991/2 was £20.2 million and in 1992/3 £30.5 million. This represents 70 per cent of the anticipated total extra expenditure on mental health, since local authorities have to find 30 per cent from their own budgets. The amount represents a significant increase in the expenditure by local authorities on mental health (£57 million in 1987/8) although it remains a very small proportion of the total (£1,552 million in 1987/8).

The grant is for revenue only; a capital loan scheme was announced a few months after the MISG circular was issued, a little late for some authorities to include in their plans for the first year.

The grant aims to target people with 'severe mental illness' who are already in contact with specialist psychiatric services and others who would clearly benefit from them, such as homeless mentally ill people. A small amount of the grant (£0.8 million in 1991/2 and £0.9 million in 1992/3) has been reserved for services for homeless mentally ill people in London. The long term future of the MISG is not known.

Social security budget

From April 1993 the social security budget to support people in residential care will be channelled through social services. Previously, health authorities could arrange placements in the private and voluntary sectors without any need to consult social services. From 1993 social services may purchase residential or social care but any community health care needed must be provided by the health authority.

Consequently, the need for local collaboration will be more urgent than ever if vulnerable people are to receive appropriate accommodation and support. Otherwise they might be at even greater risk of losing out on the basic requirements of community living.

Care programmes

The care programme requirement for people with mental health problems, introduced in April 1991 alongside the MISG, indicates the concern felt about this group. The onus is on district health authorities to draw up policies for care programmes for all in-patients considered for discharge from hospital, whether long- or short-stay, and to consult with social services before implementation. Arrangements are to be made for assessment of both health and social care needs of individuals. Users and carers are to be centrally involved in the drawing up of individual care programmes. If minimum needs cannot be met in the community, individuals should be offered a continuation of their hospital stay.

The Department of Health recommends the use of 'key workers' to monitor the agreed community services and to keep in touch with the individual and their condition. The role is described as narrower than that of a 'care manager' although some confusion must be inevitable.

In mental health, care managers, case managers, care programmes and key workers all seem to coexist. The policy of care programmes and key workers is to be implemented two years before care management is a general requirement in local authorities. The former appears to be the main responsibility of the health authority and begins from the hospital end, whereas the latter is clearly a local authority function that will involve local purchasing using a devolved budget. The term 'case management' is an earlier title for what became 'care management' in the Policy Guidance (DOH, 1990); sometimes these terms are used interchangeably. (A description by Ryan et al. (1991) succeeds in finding a niche for all three roles, but one could hardly blame local planners for being confused.)

Purchasing

One question on which there is beginning to be some measure of agreement is that of the desirability of joint purchasing. Ryan et al. (1991) suggest the development of joint purchasing consortia as one way to avoid 'cost shunting' between health and social care agencies, which might otherwise be inevitable. 'For the individual client, health and social need is indivisible' (see also *Practice Guidance for the DOH on Care Management*, SSI 1991).

Without a well co-ordinated strategy for purchasing, health and social services may find it more difficult to communicate than before, since the purchasing functions are located at different levels. Health purchasers commission blocks of service from the centre, whereas most of the important purchasing decisions in social services will be devolved down to teams of practitioners. If local purchasers were established in health authorities they might help to span the divide and provide a focal point for co-ordination.

Monitoring

Monitoring, evaluation and quality assurance are highlighted in the new policy. Key workers and care managers are to monitor and record the situation of individuals; inspection and quality assurance units are to be established in health and local authorities. External bodies such as the Social Services Inspectorate (SSI), RHAs and the Health Advisory Service (HAS) are to monitor developments and to provide help and guidance. No clear role has been identified for the views of users and carers, however, in this plethora of monitoring activity. Although they are included in the plans of some authorities for MISG projects, taking notice of users is left to local discretion.

Experiences so far

Mental Illness Specific Grant

In Scotland, the £3 million MISG (divided between eight local authorities) was allocated to 85 separate projects, £2.1 million in mental health and £0.9m for dementia services. More than half, £1.6m, was for schemes managed by the voluntary sector. The most common schemes were community development (20), day care (20), domiciliary (18), self help (13), and housing (13). Community development and housing were more common in mental health and domiciliary for dementia.

A rough estimate of numbers of people to be helped by each scheme appears a little optimistic at this stage. Estimated numbers who will receive housing and residential care total 699, with 4,200 places in day and resource centres. If half of the £3 million went to residential and housing schemes (a generous estimate) each place would be allocated an average sum of little over £2,100. This is hard to reconcile with recent estimated costs of around £14,000 per place for people resettled from hospital – although the population served may be different.

Details of the use of the first year of MISG in England were not available at the time of writing.

A sample of 14 local authorities in England were surveyed by the National Schizophrenia Fellowship (NSF) on the use of the MISG (NSF, Hogman and Westall, 1991). Most schemes funded by the grant were for adult mental health rather that dementia, with a wide range of service types represented. Day centres, including out-of-hours, domiciliary care and resettlement provision were the most common categories. Several schemes depended on the existence of empty buildings, which had to be used if possible. This could imply that resource-led rather than needs-led planning was dominant. Very few schemes were health authority managed, such as CPN teams, a finding that might allay the fears of some that the requirement to consult DHAs would lead to medically dominated care. On the other hand, the input of voluntary organisations, users and carers to the planning process in this sample was minimal, largely due to the lack of time available to construct bids. The tighter timescale for the capital loans scheme, for which 61 out of 107 authorities applied, led to even less consultation, which is unfortunate considering the more permanent and inflexible nature of capital-led developments.

A major criticism of the MISG, despite the considerable requirements for form filling and monitoring for approval by SSI and RHAs, was that only sketchy descriptions of services were provided. One application was passed that funded part of the wages for a senior social services manager and a team of four office-based planning staff. While these posts may fill important planning gaps in the authority, the use of 'ring-fenced' mental health funds for this purpose might be questioned.

Care programmes

The experience of care programmes in the first year is difficult to interpret. The first round of community care monitoring by SSI and RHAs in 1991 appears to have found satisfactory care programme policies in most authorities, according to senior management. Questioning of staff further down the organisation, however, sometimes revealed very different viewpoints and occasionally complete lack of knowledge of the existence of such a policy. The absence of additional resources to implement care programmes has been criticised by many groups, such as MIND and the NSF.

Resettlement

Some valuable experience has now been gained in the resettlement of people from long-stay hospitals. A study of 131 people resettled from two hospitals in London found some improvements in psychiatric symptoms, social contacts and social functioning (Beecham et al. 1991). The costs of community care varied enormously; there was a fifteenfold difference between the cheapest and the most expensive packages. A greater reduction in some symptoms and the broadening of social networks were generally associated with more costly care packages. The average cost of community care was roughly £14,000 per year (at 1986/7 prices), of which 77 per cent went on accommodation and living expenses and 10 per cent on day care. For this group, 52 per cent of the accommodation costs fell to the DHA, 19 per cent to the social services department, 18 per cent was spent in the voluntary sector, eight per cent in the private sector and roughly two per cent in local authority housing. In comparison, average hospital costs were approximately £15,000 and £16,300 at the same price base.

So it appears to be possible to provide suitable community care for a substantial number of long-stay residents of hospital. Many of them may benefit from a better quality of life, provided that the care arranged is of sufficiently high quality. Those who are more dependent or have greater problems will need more expensive care than others.

Health authorities may find that the costs of hospital care rise very steeply in the next few years as populations decline and unit costs go up. In addition, the introduction of capital charges to hospital costing will have a disproportionate impact on psychiatric hospitals, since the relative contribution of the capital charge to the total cost will be greater than in acute hospitals (Raftery, 1991). This may provide an incentive to accelerate hospital closures.

Good practice

Some documentation of good practice (for example Sherlock, 1991 and *Good Practices in Mental Health*) is now available; more detailed pointers are given by research studies of innovation projects. Bachrach (1980) has identified the elements that enabled schemes to reach the most vulnerable people successfully in America; Patmore and Weaver (1991) have drawn up good practice guidelines from a series of community mental health teams in England. Their suggestions include:

1. Give top priority to the most vulnerable people. Ways to target them include the incorporation of existing caseloads into new services and liaison with hospital admission wards, casualty departments and services for homeless people.
2. Provide for the full range of needs. Ensure day facilities, for example, are available and develop links with local resources.
3. Tailor the care for individuals carefully around their needs and develop services that reflect the characteristics of the local community.
4. Give the staff team clearly specified roles, monitor their case-loads and activities, and establish explicit lines of accountability. Unqualified co-workers can be a valuable asset to the team. Teams should be large enough (e.g. ten or more) to allow co-work and cover for emergencies and turn-over.
5. Provide appropriate training for all staff.
6. Monitor and evaluate the achievements of the service at intervals.

Resettlement schemes for long-stay residents of hospitals in the community have been studied by Knapp et al. (1991), some of which were markedly more successful than others.

Community-based treatment and support can be an appropriate alternative to hospital admission for some people. Methods for providing such alternatives have been described by Dean and Gadd (1989) and Marks et al. (1988). Community-based work with the families of people with long-term problems has also been shown to improve their quality of life and reduced the likelihood of relapse (Falloon, 1989; Smith and Birchwood, 199). A scheme to provide better care for offenders with mental health problems has been pioneered by Joseph (1990).

Groups of service users have contributed valuable ideas and commentary to planning groups in some areas (Beeforth et al. 1990). User groups have also provided advocacy, information and guidance to fellow users on how to present their needs to professionals (e.g. Lambeth Link).

It is important to document and build on the good practice experience of others. New schemes can then take developments a step further and spread the knowledge of what is possible more widely. These may help to overcome the substantial challenges ahead and give the policy of community mental health care the best possible chance of succeeding.

10 *Community care – change or cosmetics?* Charles Ogden

Social Services Departments in local authorities have spent 30 years developing services; initially little alternative provision existed other than particular children's residential establishments and some special services for select groups. Elected Members took decisions to develop services 'in house' and are proud of their achievements; they take a keen interest in, and seek publicity for new residential homes or day services. Need, civic pride and the evolution of the customer conscious authority have been the driving forces.

Thirty years of developing direct provision act as an impediment to preparing for the future. However, if *Caring for People* (1989) means anything, it means a change of attitude to direct provision. The most significant aspect of *Caring for People* is revealed in the concept of enabling. Local authorities should seek to free services from direct control and establish a culture that enables services to be provided and developed by others. A brief look at the history of Compulsory Competitive Tendering shows that many local authorities took very different stances towards central government's directives to contract out services, from firm embrace to outright obstruction. We can assume that this will also be the case with the enabling role.

In the drive to generate alternative provision, authorities must be flexible when considering how to specify contracts. A decision to contract out a service should not consist of a straight duplication of that which already exists. The service can be split into smaller or related parts, allowing bids from a wider range of organizations, including voluntary bodies and special interest groups. Built into the specification should be the potential for service development and change.

Clearly then, the culture and politics of each authority will dictate the depth of their commitment to the role of the 'enabling authority'. This presents a problem to senior managers, as elected members may not be prepared to 'go public' with their intentions regarding the 'enabling role', and it is crucial to the success of change to be open about where that change is taking services and, more importantly, staff. It follows therefore that openness and clarity of thought in planning are vital to success. Involving councillors and staff in the process is part of the senior managers' task.

'Enabling' should increase the range of services available, which should increase options for service users, which in turn permits a 'better fit' of services to need. In this we find a challenge: how do care managers gain access to this growing range of options? In the world dominated by internal provision, it was easy; there was an assessment – a need identified – a vacancy occurred – a service offered. No buying, no cash transaction, no problem and little flexibility. However in the new world of external provision, money must change hands, the purchaser must know how much has been spent and how much remains available to spend. That process must be thought through and budgets must be adapted to allow flexibility, in what to spend and where to spend it, at the customer/care manager interface.

Facilitating flexible budget spending at the base requires management decisions about level of provision. Full demographic information must be available to planners. Historically it has proved difficult to extrapolate exact local information from national statistics and recent challenges in the courts by service users have shown that it is imperative that senior managers and councillors have allocated adequate funds to meet assessed need.[1] Sound planning decisions require that accurate information of potential need is available. Information technology should provide this information and ensure it is readily updated through the assessment process.

Support or resistance – a success factor

The first task is one of the most problematic; how to secure the commitment of staff to work with the changes? Most people want a

1. Mr X v Hereford and Worcester County Council 'Hereford and Worcester County Council has agreed to provide (a) carer and pay Mr X £7,000 costs and £750 compensation after he won leave for a judicial review of his case in what is believed to be the first legal move of its kind'. *The Guardian*, 28 October 1981, David Brindle Social Services Correspondent

secure and lasting career. Compulsory competitive tendering has been viewed as a threat to the traditional job security of a local government career. Similarly, the 'enabling' role is seen by many as a vehicle for reducing the work force and a device for demolishing hard-won conditions of service.

There can be little doubt that in many cases the contracting out of services has had this effect. On the other hand, increasing the range of services can improve career options. Work must begin by involving staff in the process, being open about and gaining commitment to the changes needed.

It is important to have a sense of direction and share that direction by planning together. At an early stage the question everyone wants answered is 'what career options are there for me?' If planning involves an examination of the options the chance of success is greater. In drafting the specification for domestic services (separating domestic from personal care to contract out the domestic side), we found we were over-subscribed with applications from home care staff wanting to transfer into the domestic wing, contrary to expectations. Through talking with staff it emerged that they were attracted because the specification clarified their role and tasks, and guaranteed their future, or in some cases provided for the offer of redundancy. We specified a set number of hours of domestic work and established clear tasks for domestic carers. This meant staff could identify a lasting service, of a given size, and a job they could recognise. This underlines the need to help staff identify where their future lies and what choices there are.

Caring for People (1989) emphasizes the point that purchasers of service should be separated from providers of service. Changes in the departments' structure are needed to achieve that. If staff understand the difference between purchaser and provider roles, and what that means for their future, they can elect on which side of the house they want to work. *Caring for People* (1989) emphasizes that to achieve options, providers potentially should go out to alternative management. For many staff this can be positive, as local authority employment can be restrictive and proscriptive – not to everyone's taste. Change can be a threat, particularly if the planning is covert. By involving staff in the process, change can be invigorating. It does not mean fewer jobs and poorer qualify of service. Population profiles and trends in need show a greater demand for services, which means more work. If flexibility of service provision is built into contracts, it also means a wider variety of careers. I believe this will consequently improve quality. I also believe most staff will support that philosophy; it is why most of them came into the caring services.

Departmental structure

Department of Health policy guidance is unambiguous. Social service departments should seek to be 'enabling' authorities, commissioning or purchasing care services from a range of options and providers. However, it also recognizes that some service may remain with the authority as the provider. The objective is to ensure quality, safety, consumer choice and value for money. Where services do remain within the authority, that service provision should be separated from assessment and purchase. Not a cosmetic separation, but clear and unencumbered by each other's issues and processes. Failure to establish a clear separation allows the planning and commissioning process to be unduly influenced by provider issues. Providers need to have clear service objectives and specifications, a specific budget and explicit quality standards. This should be the case for both 'in-house' provision and external contractors. The latest consultation paper from the Department of Health on implementing community care (1991) reflects on the issues and suggests options for managing the council's commissioning, purchasing and providing roles. There are several running examples quoted, some of which get quite close to the government's intentions.

I think we at Bromley may have got the closest. Figure 1 is a précis of our management structure. There is a clear split in the management of purchasing and provision, all the way through to the director. We are not isolated within the authority as members and chief officers are addressing the government's consultation paper *Internal Management Implications of the Enabling Authority* (1991). The authority is actively considering a committee and management structure as outlined in figure 2. The client–contractor separation closely mirrors the purchaser–provider split in our structure. There is no unifying Social Services Committee, although Policy and Resources has a parent function. The client committee (Social Services) will draft specifications and commission services directly from the contractor committee. In figure 2 the central 'VIRES' staff indicates sections that support the 'democratic' processes.

In our social services structure (figure 1) the in-house division passes

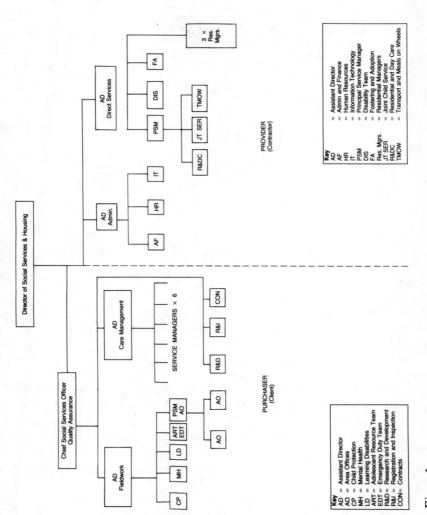

Figure 1

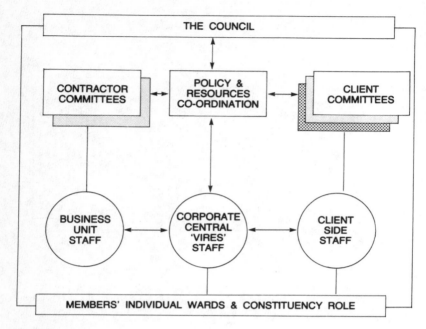

Figure 2

through the post of director, who has responsibilities for, and on, both sides of the house. Administration and direct services are clearly provider functions, and care management and fieldwork are purchasers. The chief social services officer manages the purchaser functions and is the focus for commissioning of services. In addition, in my authority, we are involved in joint planning and commissioning of services with the District Health Authority, Family Health Services Authority and Centre for Voluntary Services. We have an advantage in that we are coterminus in our boundaries. These joint commissioning activities are largely the responsibility of the chief social services officer; research and development and contracting activities therefore are also managed by that post.

The need for 'arms-length' management of Registration and Inspection is also addressed by being directly managed by this officer, though we are considering options for that service. This separation however will mean little unless people understand their roles and the philosophy, for whilst the separation is needed, communication is vital. The task for

100

managers is to ensure appropriate communication between both sides of the house, whilst ensuring that the primary roles of purchase and provision do not interfere with each other. The content and conduct of management meetings will underline the profile.

In my authority we have sought to establish care management as equal to, but different from social work. Care managers have the same pay scales, career structure and supervision as social workers. They have a workload of referrals, and assess and review each of them. However, after assessment care managers devise a 'package' of services agreed with the referee as appropriate to their needs, and cost and purchase those services. Care managers do not provide services of any type themselves, they act as agent, and if one-to-one counselling is needed, would call in a social worker to provide it.

Our structure (figure 1) illustrates one problem we have encountered and which is being recognized in several authorities. Are social workers and care managers purchasers or providers? Clearly they do purchase services in organizing a package of care, but in assessing need they are providing a service themselves. Perhaps clarity of this issue comes from being sure of terminology. I think 'purchaser' and 'provider' relate to the direct process of ensuring the needs of our customers are assessed and met. Commissioning is different from purchasing as it is understanding cumulative assessments of need and planning, and contracting to ensure services are available to meet that need. It is obvious that the commissioners need to be well informed of the identified needs in that planning process. In our structure this is achieved by senior purchasing officers being responsible for the assessment process, but clear of the provider issues. The most senior managers become planners for the service, supported and informed by the assessment of need (met and unmet) provided by care managers and social workers.

I believe this argument opens a 'can of worms' but rather than avoid it, I flag it up here. Many social workers deliver a specific purchaser type service. They assess a customer's needs and then construct a care package to meet that assessed need. If a child is placed in a residential establishment or foster placement, the package is reviewed periodically as in care management and probably little else is done in between by the social worker. Other social workers are best skilled at providing a one to one counselling service, which seems to be a provider function and very different from the former. Should the different skills and roles be acknowledged and recognized by placing social workers who assess on the purchaser side of the house, and those who provide counselling

101

on the provider side? We certainly put fostering and adoption services on the provider side.

In this structure care management has a clear role with our customers. In addition, they have an important contribution to make in the planning process. I believe this status will attract skilled people into care management, which will ensure a professional status and service.

Enabling the purchasers

In the effort to move the focus of care from residential to community services it is crucial not to restrict the freedom of the purchasers. History in social services has shown that the provision of residential services ensure their use, which in turn ensures their continuation. Care managers should be able to select from a range of options. These options will be restricted if the authority has 'ownership' of services or is contracted to purchase a fixed number of places in residential establishments. I believe this will be the case even after contracting out of services if a contract provides for the authority to continue full nomination rights. Care managers need the freedom to purchase services up to and beyond the cost of residential care. A nomination contract restricts this, since unused bed space would have the effect of reducing the spending capacity of care managers.

To give care managers real freedom to support people outside residential establishments requires offering them 'hard' cash. It is essential that care managers should know how much is available for them to spend, free of the restriction of much of that money being tied up in fixed services. Clearly there must be a range of options, including residential care, open to care managers. At the same time providers should not be dependent upon care managers for their existence. In contracting out our former homes, we have built a specification that gives us nomination rights, which reduce over a five year period. The contractors have security in that they are not 'cut free' from day one and left to trawl the market, but guaranteed business on a reducing scale whilst building up their private business. Therefore, year by year more money becomes available to care managers with which to buy options for their customers. All services when contracted out need this freedom, coupled with security, to enable options to be developed.

The advantage to care managers is the flexibility hard cash gives, but this conceals a further task, how to develop new and appropriate services. The intention is that as unmet need is identified, providers can be stimulated to develop services to meet that need. We must in consequence have a process for identifying unmet need and collating information to enable planners and commissioners. Information technology is the only process that can really satisfy this need. It is a three stage operation:

1. During assessment care managers record met and unmet need. This must include information on whether 'best option' or 'only available' service forms the care package. Care managers must have direct access to input this information.
2. The technology (both hardware and software) must be up to the task of not only holding this information in a meaningful way, but manipulating it to a high degree. There are suitable software packages on the market, some of which are very good, but as care managers become more sophisticated in identifying need, the software must be capable of development to capture and use the information.
3. For care managers to manage their budgets the system must be able to allocate costs accurately and predict expenditure over a given period. For example, if a care manager orders a domestic service such as a cleaning service for a period of time, the system should be able to show the cost at any given time, or projected, and gross up the total cost of that care manager's care packages.

Clearly there is a need for the software to have accurate base information, to allow proper interpretation of needs and trends. The time honoured extrapolation of figures from national trends is a good base. However, I think we have a unique opportunity to have exact information. The 1991 census is the most comprehensive yet completed and this information became available early in 1992. Departmental planners must not miss the opportunity to maximise the information. Work should now be in progress to consider the information the census has and glean that needed to enable our planning process and information base.

Conclusions

It seems to me that local authorities have a variety of options open to them in developing structures for community care. The main decision is, I would suggest, how far should the changes go? This is particularly crucial in establishing the purchaser/provider divide. That decision is member and chief officer led, although when it has been made, its implementation should be an open issue. We are, after all, planning around people's careers and future.

The planning process should involve staff in a proactive manner as ownership of any innovation comes from involvement and staff will not feel committed to any changes forced upon them. One of the central issues is, I believe, that the development of care management depends upon its place in the departmental structure, therefore there is a need to restructure and give care management a high profile. We must be aiming for a professional service from care managers, our service users have a right to expect that. Care management needs special training and training that is recognized as a universal qualification.

Finally, if one of the key objectives of the provision of community care is to spend money in such a way as to achieve 'best fit' of service and best value, then these two concepts must have their proper place in planning. The planning process therefore needs comprehensive information technology, which allows planners to have service usage information and population profiles. Care managers similarly need information about their spending and service usage. This is a mammoth task for both the people and the technology, but we have found that the cost is well worthwhile.

11 Budgeting, cost effectiveness and value for money Ashley Dowlen and Norman Flynn

Introduction

Social services departments and health authorities are expected to offer services to their clients that meet their needs and entitlements. The legislation assumes that previous budgetary practice emphasised the maintenance of existing services rather than the requirements of the service users. At first glance, therefore, it would seem that the whole system of allocating funds, tracking expenditure and ensuring that the best value is obtained for the money spent would need to be radically changed. However, many authorities already work in such a way as to meet the new requirements. Others have elements of the systems that will be required for the new ways of working.

The existing budgetary systems consist of two parts: elements devoted to running establishments and services provided by directly employed people, and elements that control expenditure on services provided by independent suppliers of services, whether within or outside the authorities' geographical area. Generally both elements of the budget are cash limited and managed so that no overspend occurs. In practice, if individual social workers and others are authorised to make placements in establishments that charge the authority for their services then overspends can occur. The reason for this is that if a good case can be made for the need to devote the resources, then expenditure may be committed despite the budget being already spent (Harding, 1992).

One of the purposes of the reforms is to ensure that cash limited budgets are not breached. However, simply closing budgets down when they have run out causes problems: equity of treatment is abandoned because whether a service is provided or not depends on when it is requested, rather than how much it is needed. There is growing evidence of the potential for service users to pursue entitlement through the process of legal challenge which, where successful, will diminish financial control and could distort equity as service consequently gets provided to the most persistent.

What is needed is a financial control system that gives budget holders accurate information about: the costs likely to be incurred for different elements of service, how much money has been spent and how much is still available for the services on offer.

Modifying existing systems and structures

Budgets

To make the needs-led approach work, the first modification of the budget process that needs to be made is that cash needs to be allocated to clients, or at least groups of clients, rather than to services. In practice this will be difficult, especially if the budgets available are severely limited.

The first call on any budget is the existing commitments. In any budget year it is unlikely that any authority would put whole establishments or large numbers of service providers at risk to preserve the choices available to clients or people making assessments. Even if those services or establishments are not within the ownership of the authority, contractual commitments may limit the freedom to budget for service users rather than service providers. The only exceptions to this rule are services purchased on individual transactions (or 'spot' purchases, such as paying a neighbour to provide meals). By definition, when budgets are tight the amount of cash allocated to spot purchases will be small.

If budgets are to be reorganized so that they reflect entitlement or need rather than existing service provision, new processes need to be introduced. Decision rules need to be established that allow cash to be allocated both to categories of client and to geographical areas. While such a needs-based allocation is implied by the requirement to produce a Community Care Plan, in practice most budgets are based on historical spending data rather than an analysis of the incidence of need or entitlement.

The incidence of people with an entitlement in any particular geographical area is likely to vary according to the type of need. Where there is a relatively low incidence of high cost service provision (e.g. specialised residential care) the location of budget holding would need to be at a level that allows for a reasonably planned and predicted pattern of demand. Without such sensitivity, resources will either be too scarce in certain areas or overprovided in others. Even existing decentralised budgeting systems are not sufficiently adapted to make such fine distinctions between areas and services.

Financial monitoring

If budgets are developed in such a way that larger proportions are available for buying individual care packages, the number of transactions will get very large. Information systems will have to cope with paying the individual invoices and providing the purchasers with accurate information on transactions and commitments. If a large number of transactions are for very small cash amounts (for example to pay informal carers, neighbours, local cafes) rules about spending cash will have to be relaxed or the procedures will destroy the flexibility these cash transactions are designed to achieve.

Flexibility achieved through very local, relatively informal arrangements, is likely to be constrained through issues of liability. Informal carers, for example, may find themselves liable to make income tax returns or pay national insurance or public liability insurance. As a consequence, they may decide to opt out of providing a service rather than become ensnared in bureaucracy as a result of offering to help. Liability for negligence and the resulting need to insure against claims for damages is an issue beginning to concern both purchasers and providers.

Cost effectiveness and value for money

Resource allocation

The key elements in achieving value for money in the new arrangements are an accurate assessment of the needs to be met and a system to ensure that resources are allocated to meet them. The question is: how can the social services departments make sure that the people making the assessments for individual clients and those managing services make their voices heard in the planning process? New forms

107

of relationship between purchasers and providers have the potential to eliminate a wide variety of feedback mechanisms that can exist within 'looser' partnership arrangements.

Traditionally, resources are allocated through budgets constructed on an historical basis. While changes in service provision can be made, they are usually incremental. If there are to be radical shifts in the nature of the services provided, this process will need to change. It is implied in the reforms that the budgets will be allocated to the 'purchasers' of services so that they can choose what to buy. In practice this will be difficult: budgets are likely to be committed, either to the existing directly provided services or to the contracts that have been made with external providers. Only when these commitments are met are funds available to purchase new services. During any transition to a new way of organizing funds there need to be arrangements for bridging finance. This was the case during the hospital closure programmes that transferred patients from the NHS. However, currently it seems unlikely that such funds will be available.

Budgets are also normally expressed under 'subjective headings', i.e. salaries and wages, running costs, etc. rather than in objective headings such as 'care for the elderly mentally infirm living at home'. If budgets are to be delegated to purchasers of services rather than allocated to service providers, subjective headings become irrelevant. The purchasers are interested in the prices of services, not in how their costs are constructed.

Only when the resource allocation process is changed to match the new arrangements can genuine 'value for money' comparisons be made. Even then, real choices between alternative services need to be supported by good information about availability, prices and quality.

Defining acceptable levels of quality for care services is notoriously difficult and will of course remain subjective for individual service users. There is the added danger that attempts to target or ration services will result in the withdrawal of preventive services, which may be offering better value for money for some users but which are unlikely to be provided where more acute or high dependency needs have already been met.

Monitoring

Once the plan has been translated into a budget, a different approach to monitoring is necessary. Whereas directly provided services could

108

be monitored through seeing whether the budegt was spent on what it was supposed to be spent on, once the purchaser holds the budget monitoring needs to include checking whether the required outcomes are achieved or not. It is not enough simply to see whether the money has been spent.

Trade-offs will be made by purchasers between the quantity and quality of services purchased, which implies that quality should be monitored as well as spending and the quantity of services. The different approaches to quality are discussed in Chapter 16. It is clear that any approach to quality monitoring must include assessing the service users' satisfaction with and attitudes towards the services they receive. This feedback needs to be included in any systematic decision-making about which services to purchase and from whom.

These processes are additional to the registration inspections for residential establishments and are an essential part of the value for money process.

Equity and efficiency

As well as needing information to assess the quality of care offered by different providers and to make trade-offs between quality and quantity, value for money considerations imply that equity is achieved in the allocation of services to individuals.

By equity we mean that the probability of being offered a service is the same wherever you happen to live. Technically, best value for money is achieved only when the same level of service is offered to everybody who has the same level of dependency. In practice this is unlikely to happen, not least because there will be individual variations in the care networks available to individuals with similar levels of dependency that result in different levels of service provision.

Hence, systems have to be established that produce an equitable distribution of services, both within a local authority area and between them. We know already that services vary very widely across the country and within local authority areas. Some local authorities place greater emphasis than others on social services provision. Practices with regard to the allocation of home care vary widely: the purposes of homecare are interpreted differently and the volume of service offered shows large variation.

To achieve equity would require formula-based funding, based on the incidence of need. Such a formula would have to apply both to local authority areas and within them to smaller geographical divisions. There are Standard Spending Assessments within the system for controlling spending by local authorities. Despite the system there are variations in actual spending both above and below the SSA level. Doubts have been expressed about the sensitivity of indicators used to arrive at Standard Spending Assessments for Social Services (Harding, 1992).

The other requirement would be a standardized procedure for assessments with common criteria. While this may be possible within a local authority area, it is unlikely to happen across the country. The process of assessment is not something likely to be standardized through professional practice or through a common rulebook, at least in the early years.

Even if assessment were standardized, the fact that there is an uneven distribution of services means that the outcome of an assessment will depend on the availability of services. This aspect of assessment is crucial to the success of community care. If assessments produce a statement of what a client needs, or more strongly a statement of what they are entitled to, this will not offer a guarantee that services will be provided. An assessment may simply generate an expectation or express an entitlement that is then not fulfilled.

If assessment is closely linked to resource allocation and control (i.e. assessments are made in the light of the available resources) its purpose is simply one of rationing. Authorities are adopting different approaches to the purpose of assessments.

Skills required

The community care system requires new skills, especially for those whose job it is to 'commission' or 'purchase' services. The major areas will include: the ability to utilize information technology for management accountancy and service delivery purposes; the development of quality management and performance measurement systems sensitive to user requirements; skills in contract negotiation and contract management.

The area of information technology presents the major challenge. Local authorities are unused to the levels of investment required to achieve the benefits possible from integrating a vast array of management information. Assuming the investment is available and the systems adequate for the task, there will be a major development need for managers themselves. Most social services managers are relatively unused to structured, information-based decision making on the scale envisaged. Similar developments in other, arguably less complex service sectors (e.g. retailing) have taken years to become firmly established within the organizational culture. Achieving timely, reliable, user-friendly data will be an enormous task in itself. Developing the organizational capability to utilize the data fully requires a very substantial investment in the management of change.

Quality management methods and performance measurement systems will challenge both purchasers and providers. Technical considerations aside, a major attitudinal change is required to get from 'what' to 'so what' to 'now what' in this highly complex area of management skill. Purchasers will need to develop their capability to specify appropriate quality standards and their means of assessing them. Providers will need to be able to manage to the standards and to produce sustainable evidence that their performance is satisfactory.

Negotiating and managing contracts demands a range of expertise that is probably both wider and deeper than previous 'partnership' arrangements have demanded. Central to these requirements is the change that results from the contractual process in working relationships. There is a well-recognized need to balance specification requirements with the capacity of both purchasers and providers to develop and enhance services as user expectations, organizational need and professional knowledge changes.

Many of the well-established challenges for public sector management will continue to provide the context for all levels of manager. Enthusiasm for 'general management' is being tempered by a growing recognition of the importance of the value-base of social services, the demands of rationing and targeting, and the complex legislative framework in which managers strive to deliver services to vulnerable and dependent individuals. There will be a growing need for all managers to develop a wider perspective of the environment in which they operate and to see their own role in context. In dealing with rapid change, high levels of ambiguity and increasing pressure, successful managers in the future will be those who continue to learn. Successful organizations will be those that support the culture of learning and development. Yesterday's answers cannot be relied upon to solve tomorrow's problems.

12 The management of change in service provision Ralph Davidson

Introduction

The community care legislation resulting from the Griffiths' Report (1988) and the White Paper, *Caring for People* (DOH, 1989), has initiated a period of radical change and substantial turbulence for social work. The organizational structures and processes proposed for the planning, providing and evaluating of community care services embody one of the most major redefinitions of the social work role in recent decades.

Social workers and their managers are having to struggle to adapt to new role concepts such as becoming care managers in care management systems, or procurers and purchasers of services rather than just providers, weighing the relative importance of value for money and quality of care provision, or being enablers of service users, empowering them to plan and choose appropriate, individually tailored packages of care. Moreover, these changes related to community care provision have not been taking place in an otherwise stable context. The consequences of the Children Act (1989) in England and Wales, the proposed changes in children's law in Scotland and the introduction of national standards in work with offenders are major changes in other central areas of social work provision. To respond to these legislative changes, and to capitalize on the opportunity offered by them, social work agencies have set about developing new structures and patterns of organization that will enable them to be ready to provide the new forms of service delivery that will be required of them.

All of this change, with its accompanying disruption, has come at a time when social workers were already feeling devalued and under attack. The standard of social work with children has been repeatedly questioned and assessed in recent years in child care policy inquiries, child abuse inquiries and in repeated 'exposure' by the national press of social workers who have left children to be abused in their families, or have unjustly removed children from their families when abuse was feared, or have themselves physically and sexually abused children already in their care.

In such a climate the major changes of role envisaged for social workers and their managers in the implementation of the community care legislation may be seen by some of them as offering an exciting opportunity to enter new work arenas and to master the professional challenges involved, but to others they may appear as a dreadful prospect of having to take on new areas of work for which they feel ill equipped and in which they risk being exposed to further condemnations for professional incompetence. The way in which individual social work agencies set about developing and managing their programmes of change will be crucial to the way in which their employees respond to these as ominous threats or as creative challenges. In this chapter I will consider some of the issues which need to be taken into account in the successful management of the process of change in organizations.

Change

Change is an inevitable part of daily life for us all from our earliest days and the ability to adapt to changing contexts is essential for individual and collective survival and for healthy development. Some of the changes we face will be very welcome and will be events that we have worked hard to achieve; some will be unexpected but nonetheless welcome. On other occasions changes may be very unwelcome, possibly forced on us, and have deeply distressing consequences. How individuals manage change will be affected by their perceptions of that particular change and also by their previous experiences of change. For all of us, Marris (1986) argues, some degree of resistance is an inevitable response to change: 'In this sense we are all profoundly conservative, and feel immediately threatened if our basic assumptions and emotional attachments are challenged.' All of us, as a result of our upbringing and temperament will have different positions on the attitudinal continuum of nothing ventured nothing gained and nothing ventured nothing lost. In managing our own responses to change it is important to be aware of our own natural reaction on this dimension.

Different kinds of change will be perceived as involving predominantly either continuity, growth or loss (Marris, 1986). Many changes result in continuity or incremental growth in that the needs they seek to satisfy remain basically similar. Yet it is now commonly acknowledged that even some of these changes, such as moving house or changing job, can involve considerable disruption and stress for those concerned. Other changes involve much more radical growth in which there is a much greater sense of discontinuity but where the predominant sense is still one of growth, basic confidence and expanding comprehension and competence. Finally some changes will be experienced mainly as loss, either present or anticipated, evoking all the familiar reactions to such a crisis, which have been most clearly documented in studies of bereavement (Parkes, 1972), and which can in time lead either to reintegration, new growth and secure identity or to disintegration and despair. In effect the changes we face are likely to contain aspects of each of these three patterns, i.e. continuity/incremental growth, radical growth and loss, but the one that predominates will be the crucial factor determining the degree of stress and disruption involved and the tasks the individual must accomplish to adapt successfully to their new environment.

The management of change

Sometimes change is forced on an organization by factors in its environment such as legislative, political, economic, technological or demographic changes. At other times it is voluntary and internal to the organization, arising from an awareness of innovative and improved ways of performing some of its functions. Since many of the changes resulting from the introduction of community care are of the former (enforced) variety, I shall concentrate on the mangement of these. However, it is crucial to acknowledge that this period of change can be a time when changes of the second kind should be actively sought and considered as they can play a vital role in creating the new patterns of organization and service delivery that are being developed.

For those whose principal role is a managerial one, there are three main tasks to be addressed at a time of major organizational change. The first of these is the maintenance of the existing service during the time preceding the implementation of change, the second is managing the change process and the third is managing staff through the period of change. I shall focus on the second and third of these, considering both the tasks that are involved for the manager and the skills these require.

Managing the change process

The first stage in managing the change process is **appreciating the problem** (Glennerster, 1983). In this it is important to resist the temptation to settle for the first or most obvious definitions of the problem so that one can get on with planning how to tackle it. Instead it is important to open up the process, consulting people with as many relevant perspectives as organizational resources allow. This would involve staff at a range of levels in the organization, service users and relevant people from allied, interdependent organizations, so as to obtain as broad and well informed an appreciation of the problem as possible before moving on to seek solutions. Giving time and care to this stage of the process can pay handsome dividends because if one starts with only a partial or inaccurate perception of the problem, all the work that follows will be of very limited value.

The second stage is **generating alternative solutions**. There are many techniques to enable creative thinking about new ways of working. These range from brainstorming, use of simulation exercises and games, to involving specialist consultants. Careful thought needs to be given to which are the right people from within and outside the organization to create this climate of specialist knowledge and creative thinking in which to establish a vision and then consider the means to achieve it. Those chosen to contribute should be selected on these criteria and not, as so often happens, as a product of their organizational rank. Again, time spent on generating as broad a range of potential solutions as possible will be time well spent as it will ensure that the options for action are as numerous and wide ranging as is possible.

The third stage is **assessing the implications of all the potential solutions and choosing one or more of them for implementation**. This involves considering the degree of acceptability anticipated for each solution in all those who will be involved in implementing it and, similarly, the kind of resistances it is likely to arouse in them. In other words, who will feel disadvantaged by it and in what way, and who will welcome it. Similarly, this assessment will consider the degree of advantage in each solution in relation to the amount of resources required and those available. A further important criterion in the choice between solutions is the notion of robustness (Glennerster, 1983). This means the extent to which choosing this option constrains future decisions and limits future flexibility. Where there are a considerable number of unknown or uncertain factors in the problem situation, a solution that seems most effective in the present but which majorly restricts future options may seem much less attractive to the organization than one which, though less effective in the immediate situation, leaves a far greater flexibility to the organization in its future decisions as some of the present unknowns become clarified.

The fourth stage is **developing a strategy to gain acceptance within the organization for the chosen solution**. This requires managers to understand the implications of the decision for each member of their staff. Even when managers in a hierarchical organization are in a position where they have the authority to instruct subordinate staff to implement the decision, this behaviour may lead to considerable misunderstanding, resentment and lack of co-operation. It is demonstrably more effective to devise a way of presenting the chosen solution to those who will be required to implement it in a manner that allows them to understand why it has been selected and that also minimises the extent to which they will perceive the situation as a threat or loss and maximises the advantages and opportunities it offers to them and to the service users. This is crucial in obtaining the co-operation and good will of staff, and is perhaps of particular significance when the 'optimal' solution generated has been discarded and a more robust alternative has been selected. The rationale for this choice of a less than best option may totally escape staff who have not been involved in this stage of the decision process, especially if they participated in the second stage by generating alternatives, and it will need to be clearly communicated to them all if the decision is to be seen as a rational one.

The fifth stage is **implementing the decision**. As with many other tasks the effectiveness of what is finally done is a product of the care that has gone into the planning and preparation for action. But in this stage clear communication from managers is again vital. All members of staff must understand the purpose of the new policy being implemented and exactly what is expected of each of them in their role. The means by which this will best be conveyed and understood will vary between different types and sizes of organizations and organizational

116

units, but it is a matter for which a careful strategy must be prepared by managers at all levels in the organization if the implementation is to be achieved successfully.

The sixth and seventh stages are **monitoring the new policy in practice and evaluating it**. Although they may seem fairly self-explanatory, they, like the earlier stages, need to be carefully considered and prepared. Certainly they should have been thought about at an early stage in the process so that the change can be managed in a way that builds in effective methods of monitoring and evaluation as part of the process.

Managing staff through a period of change

Although there is clearly a great deal of complex work for a manager in managing the change process, it is equally important, if the change is to be effectively delivered in the form of new services, to give great care to managing staff through the period of change (Carnall, 1990). Given the size and complexity of the changes involved in the introduction of community care and the fact that these changes are being imposed on agencies rather than initiated by them, it is not surprising that many staff will experience considerable individual and collective feelings of resistance to the changes and a wish to retain established work structures and processes.

For those staff who view the change predominantly as one of incremental growth in which they see a continuity of role, skill and professional identity, and opportunities for professional and career development, the managers' main tasks will be around information exchange and training opportunities. For those who experience it more as radical growth the managers will have to pay greater attention to supportive training opportunities, which can provide for these staff the security of developing the new skills and understanding of roles that will be required of them. Staff who see the change predominantly as loss will need greater time and different opportunities to come to terms with this loss before moving forward. The losses involved or anticipated may take many different forms, such as the loss of established professional or organizational roles, the loss of security in role whether in relation to established colleagues, premises or patterns of work, the loss of professional competence in undertaking wholly new tasks or a sense of loss of control over their work situation. Any of these, if not managed carefully, will cause anxiety, disorientation, resistance,

117

defensiveness and stress. What is essential for staff in this situation is time and space to deal with these feelings before they are required to move forward. Marris (1986) says:

'So whenever we impose disruptive changes on ourselves or others, we need to allow some kind of moratorium on other business, so that people can give their minds to repairing the thread of continuity in their attachments'.

Austin's (1984) research has shown how easy it is for senior managers, who may be the first staff in the organization to become aware of a major change that is coming, to take time to overcome the emotional impact of this and start to move forward to prepare for change but then to forget, as they convey the need for change to subordinate staff who were not yet aware of it, that they too will need time to work through their feelings. When this happens the managers will be frustrated by what they perceive as staff's unwillingness to engage in action to meet the changes while staff will experience the managers, who have come to terms with the situation, as lacking in feelings about the losses involved and uncaring about the impact of the situation on staff and service users. Thus managers' attempts to pursue rational planning with their staff will fail and a sense of alienation and conflict will emerge.

So in situations of imposed, top-down organizational change it is vital for managers to ensure that staff at all levels are informed promptly and clearly about the situation, and to maximise the possibilities for staff involvement in the whole process (Toffler, 1970). Where this is done, staff will feel valued, empowered and secure, both professionally and personally, and be most likely to identify with the change process and respond collaboratively in it.

The more staff at lower levels in the organization are kept uninformed and uninvolved the more they will feel devalued, insecure and alienated from their managers. In that situation they will tend to form small groups of like-minded people to get security and protection. Soon maintenance of loyalty to these small groups becomes more important than the change issues. Rational communication between the higher and lower levels in the organization becomes less and less possible, and instead irrationality and paranoia flourish. Eventually the possibility for collaboration in relation to the change process can become entirely lost.

Conclusion

Enforced change in an organization is often resented. Change perceived as being of a top-down pattern has the potential to go sadly wrong and to lead to a sense of mistrust, distance and alienation between senior management and lower level staff. The development and implementation of community care services will therefore be a complex issue requiring very sensitive handling by managers at all levels in social work organizations.

The task of managers in this situation is a stressful and inherently conflictual one. They must participate in managing the change process and in so doing make demands on their staff that may disrupt and endanger well established and valued practices as well as relationships within their working unit. At the same time they must manage their staff through the change process, understanding what it means for them individually and collectively, supporting them through it and protecting them against unreasonable or avoidable demands from the organization. This will require creative thinking to develop new, effective structures and processes for individual and group supervision, for work appraisal, for career planning, for team building, for training opportunities and for stress management.

In these tasks managers will require great skill in communication for it is only too easy to reach agreements in public that are not subscribed to privately by the participants (Smiley, 1982). To manage this work effectively will require a real commitment of time by managers. It will also demand a good support structure for the managers. Their position as we have just described it, on the boundary between the unit they manage and their own management system, can very easily be a conflictual and lonely one. However, if managers can be well supported, if the resources they need are provided and if they can manage their role skilfully in the ways described, this period of change in the pattern of service delivery has the potential to become a collaborative, innovative venture that can really involve people at all levels in the organization and draw them into new and closer working relationships. If it achieves this, the benefits for the organization and for the service users will be substantial.

(iii) Packaging the Care

13 *The interdisciplinary assessment of need in community care* Rosemary Bland

Introduction

Although it is local authorities who have been given the lead role in the implementation and delivery of community care, the White Paper *Caring for People* (DHSS, 1989) emphasises that assessing individual need, designing care arrangements and securing their delivery are collaborative activities to be carried out with medical, nursing and other agencies. How well agency representatives collaborate in assessment and care planning may be influenced by the degree to which organizations, particularly local authority social service/work departments and health authorities, have collaborated in the past and, more recently, in preparing their community care plans. The legislation does not oblige authorities to produce joint plans, but insists that the plans of both should be public documents and 'key contents and resource assumptions [in health authority plans] will need to be shared and agreed with the social services authority' (DHSS, 1989).

This chapter examines the current state of interdisciplinary assessment and discusses strategies that may 'ensure that all the available resources are put to best use, consumer choice and involvement are enhanced, and flexible services are provided which are tailored to suit individual need' in community care (DHSS, 1989).

The current situation

Service-led assessment

There is now abundant evidence that assessments of people requiring social care focus on their eligibility and suitability for existing provision, rather than discovering what their difficulties are (Goldberg and Connelly, 1982; Challis and Davies, 1986). This results in needs being fitted, more or less appropriately, to services, whether or not they are met in an acceptable or helpful way. The NHS and Community Care Act 1990 compels departments to change the way in which social care needs are assessed by involving individual service users throughout the process which 'they should feel is aimed at meeting their wishes' (HMSO, 1990).

Unqualified assessors

People who through age, mental illness, physical or mental disability require support in their daily lives rely considerably on their families, friends and neighbours. Requests to social work/services tend to be service specific such as home help, respite care or meals on wheels. The assessor – a home help organizer, social work assistant or probably unqualified social worker – assesses eligibility/suitability for a particular service. A home care study found assessments based on 'informal rules and established routines rather than clear policy guidance' and that 'skilled and disciplined assessment [and] careful identification of individual needs . . . were all conspicuous by their absence' (SSI, 1987).

Involvement of qualified social workers, particularly with elderly people, tends to be in crises, often concerning family support (Neill et al. 1988; Sinclair, 1988; Bland and Bland, 1985). The service response to such crises, often presenting as requests for residential care, has tended to be to provide it, with assessment limited to confirming individual suitability and 'fitness'. In one residential care study, the researcher noted that at allocation meetings, the relevance of information held by home help organizers, ward sisters or district nurses was not always recognized neither were the elderly person's strengths and aspirations' and thus 'the essence of the situation seemed to have been lost' (Neill et al. 1988).

Admission panels

Increasing demands on residential care caused social work/services to establish interdisciplinary panels with housing and health authorities to avoid 'inappropriate' placement and to control individual admission to their homes, the 'need' for residential care already defined by the referrer, though not necessarily by the elderly person themselves. Panels were seen as a way of negotiating movement of people across the so-called 'grey area' of eligibility (Westland, 1991); those deemed too fit for hospital care but too frail for residential care. Although some panels have altered their focus to meeting care needs in other ways (Davies et al. 1990), they have rarely involved direct participation by the older person or their families (their interests being represented by the social worker handling the application) which has distanced them from the assessment process.

Assessment documentation

Documentation presented to panels reflects the service-based nature of the assessment, consisting of the social worker's appraisal of the person's physical and mental state and social situation, supplemented by brief medical information from the applicant's GP. Sometimes, specialist geriatric/psychogeriatric assessment is sought, particularly if the applicant has recently been hospitalised or is thought to suffer from dementia.

In one study comprehensive medical assessment agreed by panel members but disputed between general practitioners and geriatricians over payment for domiciliary assessments was resolved by routing GPs' reports via community medicine specialists, who then summarized them for social services, avoiding the general practitioner fee (Neill et al, 1988). A Scottish study of pathways between services, found clinical medical officers mediating difficulties between geriatric and residential services (Hunter et al, 1987). Both studies illustrate the tensions and conflicts of interest between health and social work agencies collaborating in assessment and service provision.

Causes of tension and dissension

These may vary from social work/services' slow response to service requests from health professionals, reflecting departmental prioritization of work with children and social workers' reluctance to work with older people and those with learning disabilities (Challis and Davies, 1986), to the inappropriate use of the 'brief intervention model' of social work when planning long-term community support (Challis, 1991).

125

Ingredients of success

A study of projects to develop interdisciplinary need assessment in elderly people optimistically entitled *Doing It Better Together* (SSI, 1989), identified the sometimes considerable difficulties in getting representatives from housing, nursing, primary health care and hospital services to collaborate with social services staff. Each scheme developed assessment forms as a basis for joint working, only some of which reflected a needs-led approach. The researchers identified key elements in effective interdisciplinary assessment:

● motivation to develop a model
● an identified focus for joint working
● agreed clear objectives
● panels whose member status can commit resources
● reliable medical information
● administrative support and good documentation
● development of team working – understand roles and functions of other agency colleagues involved in the assessment
● client consent to confidential information sharing
● panel monitoring of their model's effectiveness
● a participative role for client and/or carer (although this did not appear to happen in any of the areas visited).

One participating local authority subsequently extended the model into setting up a Mental Health Liaison Panel. The researchers felt that panels encouraged rather then ensured interdisciplinary work at the individual client level (SSI, 1989).

The slow pace of change

A more recent SSI study of community assessment systems for all the priority groups found many key elements previously identified still lacking. Authorities had not developed formal procedures and instruments for interagency referral and assessment or defined criteria for convening interagency case conferences (SSI, 1991). Few Departments saw the necessity to formalise interagency assessment. They had not defined assessment standards within their own organizations, let alone for interagency assessment. The researchers found a continuing tendency for other agencies to request specific services rather than assessment and profound mistrust of other agencies' assessments, particularly among social work/services staff. Local authority occupational therapists were unwilling to accept their hospital colleagues' assessments and insisted on reassessing after discharge. Such interagency co-operation as existed, worked best when joint assessment was a necessity, such as the involvement of approved social workers in psychiatric settings and in multi-agency HIV/AIDS teams. Although agencies used a common language about each others' services and knew who controlled resources, they did not appear to have developed an agreed way of conveying users' social care needs to each other.

Despite the conflicts and difficulties in achieving collaboration and/ or consensus in interdisciplinary settings (see e.g. Booth et al. 1985; Brown, R. and Dalley, G. in Taylor and Ford (eds), 1989), interdisciplinary assessment and collaboration has continued to be advocated by policymakers through the establishment of interdisciplinary 'teams' for physical or mental handicap, primary health care and mental health, including dementia. Evidence for the 'success' of this organizational strategy is mixed. Progress has been made in some areas, such as in interdisciplinary projects for people with severe learning difficulties, but studies of primary health care teams have found low levels of collaboration (Huntington, 1981; Cartlidge, Bond and Gregson, 1987).

Some successful models

The care in the community projects used a range of models for assessing need including the single professional decision, interdisciplinary teamwork and the use of formal assessment schedules (Renshaw et al. 1988). Some mental illness projects, especially the larger ones, used formal assessment schedules as part of their assessment, which were useful in providing background information for interdisciplinary meetings, possibly because of their credibility with medical staff. However, when carried out in hospital, they tended to underestimate what people, particularly those with learning difficulties, could achieve in other settings (Renshaw et al. 1988).

Another means of assessing individuals with several and profound learning disabilities moving into community-based housing was developed in Hampshire and Cardiff using Individual Programme Planning, an essentially client-need based approach (Jenkins et al. 1988). This method was designed to offer a forum for interdisciplinary discussion and decision making. The project evaluators reported that 'productive working relationships with other agencies were established, the pivot of this being the IP system' (Lowe and de Paiva, 1991). However, both evaluations reported that some clients were inhibited by the size of IPP meetings and some projects sought less formal ways of eliciting clients' views and opinions (Renshaw et al. 1988; Humphreys et al. 1985).

Individuals or families requiring assistance with daily living often approach their general practitioner, reflecting the GP's pivotal role in mobilising services for patients and peoples' ambivalence about seeking social work/services help. In one study of social work and health care collaboration more than three quarters of GPs interviewed saw care for dependent members as predominantly the responsibility of families, which may explain why carers seeking help do not always get a positive response (Dalley, G. op. cit.). Their new contract may encourage GPs to advise patients, enabling their use of social services and similarly fostering relationships between general practitioners and care managers, particularly in planning elderly people's welfare (Allsop in Allen, 1991).

Practice and research-based criticisms of interdisciplinary assessments as currently experienced have found them fragmented, unco-ordinated, contradictory or repetitive in nature and service dominated (Challis and Davies, 1986). The requirement to move to holistic assessment, centred on users and carers, which aims to provide individualized rather than standardized packages of support is widely recognized (Beardshaw and Towell, 1990) but little practised.

The need for change

The new legislation assists the move to needs-based assessment by progressive separation of assessment and care planning from service provision – the so-called purchaser/provider split. This may take time to achieve. Social workers who are to be assessors and/or care managers need training for this very different approach. Moreover, the legislation makes explicit the rights of potential service users to take as full a part in the assessment of their needs as they are able, whilst emphasising carers' rights to a separate assessment if wished.

Joint training for assessors from several backgrounds may promote better understanding and agreement of each other's role and functions in community care, and avoid the overlap and duplication that can cause such bad feeling. According to Kahn (1974) the aim in interprofessional work is to 'act together' rather than 'think alike' (quoted in Hallett and Stevenson, 1980).

Social class and sex are the two most important background characteristics affecting interprofessional collaboration and efforts to communicate therefore have to be made across cultural as well as professional barriers (Hallett and Stevenson, 1980). Social workers involved in interdisciplinary assessment need to be skilful networkers able to negotiate across agency boundaries. Evidence abounds of the negative stereotypes health care and social work professionals have of each other (Dalley, op. cit.; Allsop op. cit.). In interdisciplinary relations, stereotypes provide a framework within which to conduct business, reinforce group solidarity and allow different professionals to distance themselves from others thus simplifying issues (Kahn, in Hallett and Stevenson, 1980). Unhelpful stereotyping can be broken down by different professionals being in closer contact with each other. Commonality of experience can sometimes confer similar attitudes and reactions on disparate groups of professionals but, Dalley (1989) warns, this frequently goes unrecognized and fundamental ideological differences and 'tribal ties of allegiance ensure that the gulf and concomitant hostility remain'.

The difficulties of moving towards needs-based assessment whilst encountering interprofessional resistance were recently illustrated in the Nuffield-funded evaluation of a pilot care management project (Bland, Hudson and Dobson, 1992) where care managers from nursing, occupational therapy and social work backgrounds initially had to endure considerable hostility from health and social work colleagues. Elderly clients and their supporters found difficulty expressing their needs fully, being inclined to interpret need very narrowly and to legitimate it only if related to survival. They had little knowledge about services and were reluctant to mention difficulties. Project staff feared that assessing clients' actual needs would raise unrealistic expectations, causing disappointment and frustration. In practice, they compromised, needs being identified and ways of meeting them being discussed by the care manager with the client in the light of resources currently available. This 'half-way house', 'administrative' case management (Challis, 1991) might be seen as a preliminary step towards the more radical model prescribed in the NHS and Community Care Act (1990).

If services are to adapt and change in response to user needs, assessors, users and family carers must be encouraged to convey these needs and any dissatisfactions to service planners by using the complaints procedure and by representation on Advisory Committees for Inspection Units (HMSO, 1990). Voluntary agencies may have a role in developing quality standards and complaints procedures with departments, ensuring that users' views are heeded. In an SSI study (1991), social services departments rarely visualized voluntary agency participation in the assessment process, although some agencies felt they were sometimes involved.

Improving interdisciplinary assessment

How then, can interdisciplinary assessment be improved? *The Practitioner's Guide to Care Management* suggests three ways to improve social care assessment: better consumer information, case-finding and mechanisms for assessing complex need – where interdisciplinary collaboration is often involved (SSI/SWSG, 1991).

Assessing complex need

The greatest challenge to co-operation is presented when professionals from different backgrounds, such as housing, health, education, social security and social work services, each have contributions to make to complex need assessments. At present, people with multiple needs may have these assessed by a number of different agencies in ignorance and isolation from each other. This can result in multiple assessments, confusion for the users and carers, tension between providers and overlaps or gaps in meeting needs. Giving local authorities the lead role in co-ordinating assessment and care planning is designed to overcome these difficulties. A survey of assessment systems (SSI, 1991) found little progress in the authorities studied and suggested that health, social work/services, and both statutory and voluntary housing organizations, urgently need to collaborate in assessment, acknowledging the often great difficulty in securing their involvement.

Improved interdisciplinary co-operation in assessment first of all requires an agreed operating framework. As a priority, this requires agreement on policies, procedures and standards for assessment. In order to make progress agencies need to agree:

● the purpose and desired outcome of interdisciplinary assessments
● which elements of assessed need are for social or health care

- which elements of assessment will be dealt with by which agencies
- how to resolve disputes about assessment
- whether to adopt joint documentation for assessment and how to share it
- how to monitor and revise assessment standards
- qualifications and experience of staff involved in interdisciplinary assessment
- the organizational mechanisms to enable joint assessment, such as interdisciplinary or specialist teams, interdisciplinary panels and/or case conferences and in what circumstances
- how to conduct separate assessments where users' and carers' needs conflict
- how risk will be defined, assessed and supported
- how to keep needs and preferences of clients and carers central to the assessment process
- arrangements for independent representation/advocacy for those people unable or unwilling to take an active part in the assessment.

Moving to assessment of need will involve identifying users' requirements twenty-four hours a day, seven days a week, and deciding whether a plan can be constructed to provide support. The legislation emphasizes the desirability of meeting people's long-term care needs at home or in a homely setting rather than in an institution. After April 1993, all those needing assistance with independent sector residential or nursing home fees will have been assessed by social services as requiring this level and type of care. Hitherto, people entering private and voluntary sector homes have done so unassessed, using social security funding. There is great emphasis on the need for care plans to be cost-effective in meeting individuals' assessed needs – a powerful argument for having the assessment and care management roles vested in one individual with knowledge of service costs and access to a budget to purchase care. This enabled the Thanet case managers to become very innovative and flexible in meeting the needs of clients in that project (Challis and Davies, 1986). As needs changed over time reassessment ensured that the care plan continued to meet clients' requirements.

Conclusion

The history of interdisciplinary co-operation shows its extreme variability. Sociological analysis has documented structural and professional obstacles to co-operation and collaboration that bedevil attempts to provide the 'seamless service' to users that policymakers demand. Successful interdisciplinary assessment and care planning has been aided by agreeing the goal of the assessment, the existence or development of a documentary framework for carrying it out and who will be responsible for providing the medical, functional and social care assessments of a person's needs. Organizational frameworks such as specialist social work or interdisciplinary teams, case conferences and panels have sometimes enabled different professions to collaborate successfully. However, it is clear that, like the process itself, better interdisciplinary collaboration in complex assessment will take time.

14 *Matching needs and resources – manager or broker?* *Pete Ritchie*

None of the ideas in *Caring for People* (DOH, 1989) has generated so much comment, guidance and professional anxiety as the proposal to cast assessment and care management as 'the cornerstone of community care' (para.1.11). Yet three years after the White Paper, while inspection units, contracts and community care plans have come to pass, there are few local authorities with a care management system in place that remotely resembles that described in the recent guidance (SSI, 1991). Hundreds of demonstration projects, but no cornerstones.

Care management is defined in this guidance simply as 'the process of tailoring services to individual needs'. To a newcomer, it would seem odd that this was a new idea in human services, but those with more experience know that the tradition of tailoring in services owes more to Procrustes than to Savile Row.[1]

Matching needs and resources – the problem

While few people think that all the shortcomings of the current services could be removed simply by a redistribution of the existing pot of resources, there is a widely-held conviction that the resources available are not well-matched to the needs of people who rely on services (Audit Commission, 1986). Opinions diverge, however, when it comes to explaining the mismatch and how to resolve it. These schools of thought can be crudely summarized as the reformers and the radicals.

1. Procrustes was a legendary Greek robber who used to make a bed for all his 'guests': if they were too tall he cut their legs to fit; if they were too small, he stretched them

The reformers advocate improving the services available through training, quality assurance, contracts, inspection, etc. and improving the match between individuals and services by greater accessibility, better assessments and smoother co-ordination.

The radicals argue for fundamental change, in which care management is at best a distraction:

> 'it is simply not enough for brokers, care managers or any other agent to potter about in the existing mish-mash of inappropriate and inadequate services with a view to helping disabled people to piece together some kind of a survival plan for existing in a hostile world. We have been there for far too long' (Davies, 1990).

This chapter assumes the reformist framework and analyses models of care management within this context; how should care management contribute to improving the match between resources and needs?

Matching needs and resources – causes and remedies

A number of strategies are proposed, based on assumptions about the way community care is currently provided.

Provide better information

'The services are there, but the people who need them most don't get them because they don't know about them.' Evidence for this view may be derived from the fact that services frequently 'discover' people who could use some considerable help but who do not appear on anybody's list, or from the fact that using one service (such as sheltered housing) is a better predictor of using another service (such as home care) than any more objective measure of disability. Even where people are in contact with services, they may get poor information about service alternatives or about access to resources such as the Independent Living Fund.

While there is little doubt that the quality of information given to 'customers' and 'potential customers' is still unacceptably poor (particularly in the public sector), we should not assume that those customers know nothing about services. Sometimes people clearly perceive that asking for services may mean asking for social stigma, loss of autonomy, denial of cultural values, or even overt racism. If we are to promote a product better, it helps to have a better product to promote.

Assess 'real need' better, so we can fit services to people not the other way round

On this view, the services that people need are not there – or not there in sufficient quantity – and they will only be provided if we carefully distinguish what people really want from what they can actually get at present.

There are two versions of this argument. One suggests that we can put together individualized packages of service by tapping into resources outside the service system, so instead of getting a place at a day centre, an older person might spend time with a companion pursuing a lifelong interest in train-spotting or horse-racing.

The other version suggests that this 'service-independent' assessment of what people need is used both to argue for an appropriate response from service providers to each individual's needs and to inform strategic planning and purchasing by the commissioning agency (Smith, in Peck, 1991). These arguments are picked up again at the end of the chapter.

Allocate and ration services more efficiently

On this view, existing services could be used more efficiently if the right people got the right amount of each service. This can be done in various ways:

- The tariff for access to services can be raised. Older people who ten years ago would have been offered a few hours free home help service for their housework now are ineligible for a local authority service in many areas and may instead be offered a list of reputable agencies. Only older people who need personal care qualify for the home care service and are usually expected to pay at least something towards it.
- Lower-paid workers can extend their skills through in-service training and substitute for professionally-qualified staff.
- Productive 'contact time' can be increased by allocating staff to a small geographical patch and organizing their work by task (getting someone up and giving them their breakfast) rather than by a time slot (9–11 am three days a week).
- Cheaper options can be substituted for more expensive ones. If someone can be maintained at home for less than the average cost of a residential care place, that is the preferred option.
- More frequent review of the appropriateness of the service provided.

Some people keep on getting a home help long after they have recovered from the illness that caused the initial need; others get 'stuck' in high cost residential care when they want to move to a more independent setting.

Co-ordinate services better around individuals

While the 'right' person may be getting the 'right' services, they may be provided in a disorganized or inconvenient way. For example:

> 'The home help often arrives too late in the morning to help Mr Smith get ready for the day centre bus, which comes for him every Thursday. This takes so many detours that the five mile journey takes 90 minutes. Mr Smith then gets back too late to catch the mobile library and is usually too tired by the evening to get out to the pub for the dominoes night'.

People who rely on many sources of formal and informal support may easily be pulled in different directions, and may find it difficult to organize the help provided rather than be organized by it.

Raise the quality of service to individuals

Although people may be getting a service that sounds like it will meet their needs, often this service is actually very poor, and public money is being wasted on a poor quality response to people's needs. For example, within a residential setting people's preferences and requests are routinely ignored, their physical care is provided in a clumsy and disrespectful way, or they are unable to maintain contact with old friends.

While the way to improve the quality in the long term may be through the contracting mechanism at the local authority level, some improvements may be possible through individual service agreements drawn up between the individual and the service provider and monitored regularly by or with someone external to that service. These diagnoses are not new, but care management claims to offer a way to administer the remedies.

Enter the care manager

The concept of care (originally 'case') management, as used in *Caring for People* and subsequent guidance, has fuzzy edges. In part, this is to allow it to address all of the issues identified above.

The practice guidance claims the benefits of care management range from 'a needs-led approach to assessment and the use of resources' through to 'more responsive services', 'a wider choice of services', 'greater continuity of care and greater accountability to users and carers', 'better integration of services within and between agencies' and 'a way of meeting the needs of disadvantaged individuals more effectively'. A powerful tool indeed, if it can live up to all these expectations.

Case management originated in the USA around 'multi-problem families' (Weil, 1985) and a brokerage-type model, but has diversified to encompass an enormous variety of models, with continuing disputes both there and here about what case management really is, and how to do it best.

The official guidance has settled on defining care management in terms of seven core tasks:

● publishing information
● determining the level of assessment (following referral)
● assessing need
● care planning
● implementing the care plan
● monitoring
● reviewing

The guidance recognizes that there are many different ways of getting those tasks done.

Provider-led care management

Broadly speaking, care management practice can be provider-led, purchaser-led and user-led. This does not mean that only the interests of one party are recognized; but that practice is influenced by a particular ethos and line of accountability. Under each of these three headings, there are innumerable variations on a theme (Palmer, 1991).

Examples of provider-led practice in this country include child-centred casework, individual programme planning for people with learning disabilities, community mental health teams and some intensive home support projects for older people. The focus is on co-ordination and co-operation between professionals and agencies around individuals who need a variety of services.

Good practice in these contexts will typically include some form of holistic assessment, the participation in all stages of subject and their carers, exploration of options followed by the negotiation and implementation of an agreed care plan; and a built-in system for monitoring and review.

While in the past many of the professional staff involved may have been employed by the purchasing agencies, their perspective has been predominantly 'clinical' rather than managerial or financial. Such staff might argue that assessment is not a simple process, divorced from the provision of services, and that to introduce a second-tier care manager who has no clinical role with the service user is a triumph of bureaucracy over commonsense.

Purchaser-led care management

Purchaser-led care management focuses on the rational allocation of resources to individuals. Decisions about what services someone needs and can have are made by someone in the purchasing authority, not by a service provider. The agreed services may then be negotiated, co-ordinated and monitored by the same practitioner.

This model of care management is a function of the system as a whole, not something that just happens to people whose situation is complex or high risk. In other words, decisions about eligibility for services and whether someone needs to have their care managed are themselves part of the care management system.

The government's enthusiasm for this approach derived originally from two sources. Fifteen years ago, the Kent experiment showed that by delegating authority to case managers to use two-thirds of the cost of a residential care place it was possible to support frail older people at home, despite major gaps in the formal service system (Challis, 1986). Ten years later came the major political agenda of splitting the purchaser and provider roles, not just in community care but also in housing, health and education. Purchaser-led care management appeared to offer not only greater efficiency of resource use, but also a way to divorce purchasing from provision at the front line as well as at Headquarters.

User-led care management

User-led care management starts with the person – their situation, ambitions and obstacles. Care managers are expected to have, as far as possible, no conflicts of interest; in other words, they are not also accountable for selling services or for balancing budgets. CHOICE – the care management project in North London for people with physical disabilities – was one of the first examples in this country. This form of care management has also been described as service brokerage (although some proponents of service brokerage (Brandon, 1989) argue that this is a misnomer and that service brokerage means not just accountability to, but direct management by the user and/or family). The care manager negotiates with service purchasers and/or providers with and on behalf of the service user, and offers information, continuity and advocacy.

These broad categories can be linked back to the Maxwell criteria for quality in Chapter 16. Provider care management should promote effectiveness, purchaser care management is intended to ensure equity and efficiency, and arguably user-led care management is more likely to promote acceptability and appropriateness.

A discrete role, or a set of tasks?

Like any priesthood, community care has its theological debates. One continuing controversy has been around the question 'Should you have one person who is a "care manager" or is care management a set of tasks that can be done by different people at different times?'

The 1990 Department of Health guidance is unequivocal: 'Care managers should in effect act as brokers for services across the statutory and independent sectors' It goes on to say 'care managers need not be employed by a statutory authority: for instance staff in voluntary bodies may be the best qualified to do this, particularly where service users have specialised or complex needs'.

The SSI 1991 guidance, however, concedes that the model of care managers with unambiguous 'caseloads' and devolved budgets is probably not generalizable. 'What authorities and agencies face in generalising care management to all users is not the development of one model but a range of models, suited to the type and level of users' needs. This will require the development of selective criteria to determine the allocation of users to different arrangements' (p.74).

The social entrepreneur, the white knight, the hero-innovator has been replaced by care management – the system(s).

However, once the thread of a single named worker has been

dropped from the list of core tasks, the concept of care management becomes even more slippery. What is left is that – whether or not the staff who undertake assessments also take purchasing decisions or also undertake care planning or service provision – assessment of need at an individual level for services funded by the local authority is to be done by the local authority.

There has been no suggestion of compensating for this centralizing of authority by giving users themselves the money once the assessment has been done and the delegation to practitioners of real cash rather than simply authority to commit service resources now seems optional.

Care managers – or functionaries?

One of the intentions of *Caring for People* was to 'give people a greater individual say in how they live their lives and the services they need to help them to do so' (p.4); what is implied by the guidance is a system where local authority practitioners act as gatekeepers to all community care services.

Rationing has to happen somewhere, but there are two dangers in it being done on a case-by-case basis by people at a low level within the rationing authority. The first is that of excessive caution and restrictiveness, as happened with the introduction of the Social Fund. The second is the allocation of standard solutions, especially where marginal costs are low; it is hard to see a professional incentive to be imaginative when those making the assessments are primarily functionaries of a procedure-driven local authority.

There are alternatives to case-by-case rationing. Service specification can be used to ensure that, while service users have direct access to a range of providers, those providers demonstrably focus their resources on the people who need them most. Another approach is independent assessment of need, linked to cash payments as with the Independent Living Fund.

A combination of these two approaches, the first for 'collective' services such as shared housing, supported employment, day centres, etc. and the second for individual services such as personal and domiciliary care, could be used effectively within the overall parameters of the community care plan.

In rejecting the ideas of entrepreneurism and brokerage and clinging to an 'authorization' approach, the guidance has set care management up as an essentially conservative force. However, there is little danger of the guidance being implemented in a systematic way. Given the demands of community care planning and contracts for services, and the uncertainties surrounding the transfer of resources from DSS, the council tax and the move to single tier authorities, few authorities are likely to attempt to set up a comprehensive care management system in the near future.

The return of the broker

So there may still be room for semi-autonomous agents to operate at the edge of the system, doing deals for individuals and/or keeping the purchasers and planners informed about the gap between aspirations and resources. The focus of the brokers' work may be anything from helping older people to maintain ties and connections with their community, to helping people leave psychiatric hospital and get themselves back on their feet. A wise purchaser will nurture and learn from such small initiatives, even if they reach relatively few people.

But the bulk of care management for the foreseeable future will be done not by the handful of brokers, fixers and care co-ordinators operating at arm's length, nor by the full-time assessors based in social work departments, but by the providers, whether in-house or independent, offering long-term home care, day services and supported housing.

Helping these services to become more responsive and ensuring that they reflect the values that should be at the heart of community care is a better strategy for improving the match between needs and resources than embarking on the wholesale implementation of care management along the lines now suggested in the guidance.

15 *Safeguarding the carers* Jill Pitkeathley

Carers and their circumstances

The definition of community care given by Professor Kathleen Jones
in 1972 is justly famous.

> 'To the politician community care is a useful piece of rhetoric, to the
> sociologist it is a stick to beat institutional care with; to the civil servant it
> is a cheap alternative to institutional care which can be passed to the local
> authorities for action, or inaction. To the visionary it is a dream of a new
> society in which people do care; to social services departments it is a
> nightmare of heightened public expectations and inadequate resources to
> meet them. We are only just beginning to find out what it means to the old,
> the chronic sick and the handicapped'.

What would strike anyone very forcibly now though is the lack of
reference to carers. In fact, if we were to be guided only by the
literature and policy documents of recent years, we might imagine that
caring had just been invented – that carers sprang into being sometime
during the mid-eighties. Since the word carer is sometimes rather
loosely used to include professional carers, such as nurses and social
workers, it should be defined here. A carer is someone, usually but by
no means always a relative, whose life is in some way restricted by the
need to take responsibility for the care of another person who has a
physical or mental disability or is ill or frail through old age. Using this
definition there are 6 million carers in Great Britain, 1.7 million of them
are living in the same household and 1.4 million are spending more
than 20 hours a week in caring duties. Seventy five per cent of all carers
are looking after someone elderly and 42 per cent are themselves over
retiring age (Green, 1988).

142

Although we have only recently become aware of these statistics, of course carers have been in existence as long as relationships themselves. However, two developments have brought them into greater prominence in recent years. The first is the rapidly increasing number of older people in our society. Although you do not necessarily need more care just because you are old, it is undeniable that after 75 years or so your chances of managing at home without help lessen considerably. The second factor in bringing carers more prominently into focus is the commitment of successive governments over a period of about the last 30 years to a policy of so called 'care in the community'. Care in the community largely means care by the community and what is the community but a member of your family, a neighbour or friend? Most carers do not want to stop caring, they do what they do out of love or duty and the moral obligation to care for your family still seems to be strong in the United Kingdom (Pitkeathley, 1989). In the course of this enormous contribution carers are making to community care, and often the job they do is harder, more stressful and more time-consuming than any paid employment, carers suffer a variety of problems – financial, practical and emotional (Parker, 1990).

As far as finance is concerned, the support received by carers is minimal. There is the Invalid Care Allowance, which is paid directly to carers, but out of the 6 million carers only about 170,000 receive it and when they do it is only £32 per week. Caring largely takes place in poverty, not only because the allowances are inadequate, but because caring itself is expensive: you may need extra heat, light, special kinds of food, extra transport that you may have to pay for and so on. In addition to this there are the opportunity costs for carers: many of them give up work to become carers so not only do they lose their current income, but they lose potential income for the future, which means they have little chance to build up the kind of financial reserves that they themselves need at a later stage in their life and, of course, they lose promotion opportunities at work too.

Then there is a whole range of practical problems which carers face (Carter et al. 1990), such as dealing with incontinence, getting someone out of bed in the morning who is virtually immobile, managing to go out shopping, managing to snatch a night's sleep or even an hour's sleep at a time. We must remember that many carers are caring 24 hours a day, 7 days a week, and the range of practical problems they suffer is really enormous.

And then perhaps the greatest problem of all for carers are the emotional difficulties that occur as a direct result of caring. Caring isolates you. It often means that you are isolated not only from your community but from the rest of your family. There may be problems of resentment within the relationship and there will almost inevitably be the problem of the carer feeling guilty. Somehow or another when you are a carer, no matter what you do you feel you are not doing enough. We have to remember a central fact about caring is that it takes place within an existing relationship. If you were not in the relationship with the person needing care you would never become their carer. The nature of the relationship before the caring began will often inform the relationship during caring and we all know that relationships within one's family or one's circle of friends are extremely variable and not always easy.

Fifty eight per cent of carers are thought to be at risk of physical or mental illness as a result of their caring and anyone who has ever sat in on a carers' group will have been very much affected by the kind of distress carers bring into that situation. It should not be forgotten though that, as well as distress, caring can bring joy, love and reward.

What carers need

It is not difficult to get agreement about what should be done for carers. Policy makers, service providers and professionals and, indeed, carers themselves, will quickly agree the following (Twigg, 1990; Haffenden, 1990).

We should recognize and acknowledge the contribution made by carers. They should be involved in planning services and be treated as full and equal partners. Both carers and cared-for persons should have a choice and adequate information on which to base that choice. Practical help and services should be flexible enough to take account of the different needs of individuals, including ethnic and cultural differences, and they should be available as part of the carers' ordinary life, not just in emergency at a time of crisis. Carers should not be obliged to take on the caring role but should be able to say no if they wish. Carers should have an adequate income and should not be penalized financially for taking on the caring task.

Reaching agreement on these principles presents no great difficulty. Turning commitment into reality, however, is usually much more

difficult. It was extremely important that Sir Roy Griffiths acknowledged the importance of carers in his seminal report *Agenda for Action*
(1988) and that the subsequent White Paper (1989) followed suit.
However, we should never forget Sir Roy's cautionary note when he
remarked that no legislation was going to transform the lives of carers
and that the best that we could hope for was that we might turn the
intolerable into the reasonably tolerable.

Because many existing services have been developed to meet the
needs of elderly people living alone, they are often not suitable for
carers. The new community care legislation offers specific opportunities for adapting or modifying existing services for the benefit of
carers. It will be particularly important to bear in mind the following
four points.

1. **Recognition.** Carers are expected to take on great responsibility and
to provide huge amounts of care with their own need unacknowledged.
Too long the presence of a carer in the household has been the signal
for service deliverers to breathe a sigh of relief and think that that
was one problem they could ignore. The assessment processes that
come into operation in 1993 may give more opportunity for the
carers' situations to be considered together with those of the cared-
for persons, and for the carers to choose whether to continue the
caring role or not. If, for example, carers want to continue working
at a much liked or much needed job, that is what they should be
helped to do. It is not enough to start from the premise that once
carers give their jobs up, then help will be provided. Neither is it
for anyone else to make a judgment about whether carers should go
on working or not. They themselves should decide and support
services should be arranged accordingly. The aim should be to work
towards partnership in caring, with carers being seen as at least equal
partners not passive recipients of services. New community care
arrangements, if properly implemented and adequately funded, do
provide a better opportunity than we have ever had before for carers
to be able to make decisions about the caring process within a
framework of discussion, negotiation and choice.

2. **Information.** Carers need information badly about the services
available in their area, about the benefits to which they are entitled,
about being a carer, about changes in legislation and, if appropriate,
about the condition of the person for whom they are caring. A

145

saturation policy is necessary when trying to get information over to carers. You have to use not only every professional and voluntary agency with whom they could come into contact, but also make information available in different places in different forms, in everyday language not professional jargon, in a range of languages and to present the material as accessibly as possible. However good written material is, many people have difficulty in absorbing things that must be read and here the local radio and television can be extremely effective. Everybody who is involved with carers needs to operate a 'think carer' policy, so that providing information is not seen as the responsibility of one organization or one person. It should be something that everybody remembers to do and everybody should be aware that giving information is not something done once, but that it needs checking and re-checking as people's needs change.

3. Practical help. New community care arrangements should enable better practical help to be available to carers. A comprehensive service of practical help would provide assistance with domestic and caring tasks, aids, equipment and transport, and would also offer up to date information about what is available. Though little progress has been made as yet, I hope that in the future policy statements will acknowledge that caring commonly involves heavy physical work and 24 hours a day attention. Too often out of hours services are simply not available. Those professionals charged with providing such help should be able to carry out the tasks carers want and at the time carers want. They should be willing to work closely with individual carers to ensure that they can provide help appropriately. Carers should, of course, be consulted about the range of practical help provided, including the amount, kind and suitability.

No acknowledgement of carers' needs for practical help can ignore the need for respite care. Some time off often enables carers to carry on. That time off must not be given at the behest or in the way most suitable for the service provider, but rather in a way directed at meeting the carers' own needs. This means that respite care must be offered in flexible ways. It must include sitting services, night sitting services, information schemes, day care, short stay places, family care schemes, befriending schemes and holidays. At present, half of those caring for more than 20 hours a week have never had a break since they started caring. Respite care must encompass any means by which carers can be given a temporary break from their caring responsibilities. Opportunities for a break must be provided for people with a wide range of care needs without prejudice to their dignity and independence and without discrimination on grounds of race, age or gender. Both the carer and the person with disabilities should be involved in decision making about the help they require and can accept. Some of these provisions do already exist, but in many areas the provision for respite care and for practical help in the home has grown up in an uncoordinated way. Policies need to be extensively overhauled. Thus far practical help for carers is sparse and has often been marginalized. Now that the government's White Paper on Community Care and subsequent legislation (1990) has explicitly moved them to the forefront of the debate, services that provide practical help at home to carers, including respite care, must be underpinned by a revitalized management approach. Local authorities are putting into place clear systems of community care planning and individual assessment, accompanied by area-wide consultation, effective multi-disciplinary working and declaimed quality standards. The way in which these operate over the next nine or ten years is going to be vital in providing real care for carers at home.

4. Emotional support. Until very recently, carers went completely unrecognized in our society (Arber and Ginn). The word 'carer' has only just appeared in the Oxford English Dictionary, though at least it is less frequently misspelled 'career' now. The result is that carers have felt undervalued, ignored and isolated. As one carer said 'It hurts me when I think of how I am taken for granted. I am not a wife in any sense of the word, but simply an overworked house-keeper. Very much his world, as far as I am concerned. I have no status whatsoever. I hope I don't sound terrible, but when no one values you it makes you feel and believe that you have no value at all.'

Clearly some of these services need extra resources. It would be a great deal easier to provide carers with the services they so much need and deserve if money and staff were more plentiful. However, it is too easy to let service providers off the hook through this argument, since many of the improvements that need to be made for carers are not about resources at all, but about attitudes that need to be changed and skills that must be developed if a better deal for carers is to become a reality. Since carers have only just been recognized as a client group with needs different from those of the people they care for, many professionals who act as gatekeepers to services may be at a very early stage in developing the necessary skills. Moreover, it is well known that attitudinal changes are the hardest of all to achieve.

Responding to carers and the new community care arrangements

The following points may be useful to bear in mind:

1. Carers neither know nor care who provides a service. It may be very important to others, especially the providers themselves, whether a service is provided by health, social services or the voluntary sector. Few carers will understand the difference between these agencies and will care even less. What matters to a carer is that the service is reliable and flexible and that they do not feel demeaned by using it.

2. Most carers receive no services at all. Even at the heaviest end of caring – more than 20 hours a week – two thirds of carers receive no help at all. So it is not just a question of re-arranging the delivery of existing services but of a radical new look at the needs of carers.

3. The needs of the carer and the needs of the cared-for person are not always the same. Indeed, they may often be in conflict. This means that professionals will in future be called upon to play a negotiating role between carer and cared-for person that is unfamiliar to them. What has to be borne in mind is that the relationship between carer and cared-for person has often none of the negotiating 'rights' within it that most of us expect within our normal relationships. This may be because one or other of the partners has given up the idea of any negotiation in the interests of a quiet life or perhaps because the cared-for person has some kind of illness or disability that impedes their ability to discuss and reach agreement. The professionals making assessments will need to develop skills in helping them with this aspect if carers' needs are to be addressed in the new community care arrangements.

4. Professionals will have to develop a whole new understanding about what carers actually need. Many people are very nervous about asking carers what they need for fear of what they may demand.

Because the numbers of carers is so large, social services departments may feel real fear about what the Carers' National Association calls the 'opening the floodgates' syndrome. Yet research consistently shows that carers in fact ask for less than service providers think they will want. What they do ask for though is often different from what is on offer. A recent letter to CNA, for example, was from Anne, who suffers from celebral palsy and is in a wheelchair but who, in spite of her own disability, is the carer for her mother, Olive, also a CP sufferer and also in a wheelchair. Olive needs personal care and cannot wash, go to the toilet or dress herself without help. Anne, however, is perfectly happy to provide this help. What they both find difficult is housework and what they need from the social services department is help with the housework once a week, since they find vacuuming from a wheelchair difficult. The SSD cannot provide this because their home help service has been changed to a home care service. Instead, they have offered this family eight hours personal care, which they do not want.

Conclusion

Really listening to carers can make sound economic sense, but it does require the development of new skills and new attitudes that may not be present in professionals at present. The need to develop these is urgent and there are clear implications for the training of those professionals who work in all agencies involved in community care. Nor will all the changes be required on the side of the professionals. The carers too will need to become more assertive and bolder in exercising their political power. There is now evidence that the carers' movement is growing more vocal. Most carers do not want to stop caring, but the love and obligation they feel to the people they care for should no longer be an excuse for ignoring their needs.

(iv) Monitoring the Care

16 *The process of quality assurance*
Pete Ritchie

Introduction

Quality assurance is fashionable just now in community care because it promises something to everyone. For central government, the demand for better quality public services has been a convenient battle cry – but has also touched an important chord with many of those on the receiving end. Major purchasers and funding agencies want to be sure that what they are buying is good enough. Quality assurance offers providers a way of demonstrating the quality of what they do to purchasers, and supports effective management. For staff, quality assurance can open channels for consultation and discussion, and provide a clear framework for day-to-day practice. For users of services, it offers a guarantee that the service they use is 'up to standard'.

All these groups have a common interest in improving the quality of community care services. However, the quality assurance process can also be used for other purposes. For example, it can be used to shift responsibility for quality to a lower level without shifting control of resources; issuing specifications for brick quality without issuing straw. It can be used to pretend to yourself and others that a poor service is now high quality because it has a process of quality assurance; this can best be described as 'quality reassurance'.

The rest of this chapter outlines the issues in using quality assurance constructively, but like any other 'systemic' process quality assurance influences the whole culture of the organization and, if taken seriously, will mean changes in role, power and status.

What is quality assurance?

Like any emerging field, quality assurance is riddled with discussions of terminology and definition. In this chapter, quality assurance is used as an umbrella term to describe any systematic, cyclical process that *defines* the intended quality of a product or service, *compares* what is produced or provided with the intended quality, and implements *changes* in order to improve the quality of the product or service. This process can be respresented diagrammatically as shown in Figure 3.

Quality assurance in community care

Two levels

Quality assurance in community care operates at two distinct but interrelated levels: the programme (a staffed house, a day centre, a family support service) and the system of services. The criteria for quality, the methods of assessment and the strategies for change may be different in important ways. A parallel can be drawn with a major construction venture such as the Channel Tunnel. The quality of the

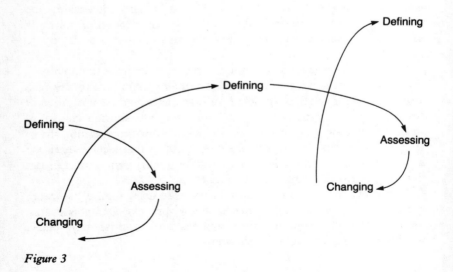

Figure 3

component parts has to be assured, but the quality of the whole is not determined simply by the quality of the parts; if the Channel Tunnel turns out to be in the wrong place, the wrong size or too expensive, it is not the fault of the firm that makes the ventilation fans.

At the system level, the purchaser of service – and thus indirectly the community – needs to know about the quality of the whole system of provision; how well it hangs together, and whether as a whole it delivers what it is supposed to. Maxwell (1984) defined quality in terms of appropriateness, acceptability, equity, accessibility, effectiveness and efficiency; these domains fit most comfortably with quality assurance at the system level, the level at which the Audit Commission typically operates.

This chapter focuses on quality assurance at the programme level – and within this the issue of delivering quality services to individuals with different requirements and different values. The 'systems' issues are equally significant, because community care creates opportunities for redrawing boundaries. As the lead agency for community care, the Social Work Department has to look at quality in residential care in the context of the quality of the wider system of housing and support for people with special needs.

A variety of approaches

At the programme level there are many different approaches to quality assurance. One thing that distinguishes these approaches is who takes primary responsibility for these three processes.

In a *regulatory* approach to quality assurance, quality is defined and standards set externally; external inspectors assess how far standards are being met and make recommendations for change. This model has been criticized as ineffective along the general lines of 'You can't inspect quality in'. Lord Cullen (1990) makes a similar point in his critique of North Sea oil safety arrangements and proposed a shift of responsibility for safety from the inspectorate to platform operators within a jointly agreed framework.

In a *military* or *hydraulic* approach to quality assurance, senior management take responsibility for all three stages – defining quality, assessing performance and making changes (or, more usually, blaming the workers). Pyramid building is an early example of this approach, which relies on a stable external environment, an unambiguous task, omniscient managers and compliant or expendable staff. This model is likely to be ineffective when the environment is changing, and tasks are both complex and not clearly defined – as in the current community care scenario. Experience in quality circles (Robson, 1984) shows clearly that frontline workers are willing to invest time and energy in defining and solving quality problems that are invisible or insoluble if power is retained at senior management level.

In a *contractual* approach to quality assurance, the purchaser specifies quality and the provider delivers to the specification. Assessment of performance may be done wholly by the purchaser (the man from Del Monte says yes) or primarily by the provider. In the latter situation, the purchaser may be as interested in checking the robustness of the provider's internal quality assurance system as in undertaking direct 'hands-on' assessments of quality. This accounts for some of the popularity of externally validated standards such as BS5750, which guarantees to the purchaser that the provider has a thorough, functioning quality assurance system.

In a *collaborative* approach to quality assurance such as Quality Action Groups (Ash et al. 1991) service users work with frontline staff and managers to define quality, assess service performance and effect change.

The quality assurance model in use in any one organization is likely to contain a mix of these approaches; fostering collaboration but within constraints imposed by the purchaser, managing the tension between standardization and diversity. There is no single best model that will suit every organization at every level now and in the future – no 'holy grail' (Smith and Mansell, forthcoming).

Defining quality in a community care service

Defining quality in community care is a value-laden activity. The definition of quality depends on the assumptions made about the proper role of disabled people in society. It is also a political activity. Influencing what counts as quality has implications for how resources are used, within and between services.

There is no consensus about what counts as good community care. Present care services have evolved from services specifically designed to segregate people with disabilities as 'social casualties' and to provide the minimum acceptable levels of maintenance. While the language, beliefs and intentions of practitioners may have evolved, the service models and frameworks have changed much more slowly and erratically.

A 'prescriptive' view of services sees professionals as the arbiters of need and the core problems being about ensuring 'accurate' assessments and equitable rationing of resources in relation to those assessments. A 'free market' view of services sees users as the arbiters of need and the core problems being an equitable distribution of disability income and the development of a diversity of services for people to buy. A 'social change' view of services sees the interaction between users and society as the key issue and the core problems as helping generic services and structures to become inclusive and helping existing services to keep people in society rather than keep them out.

These contrasting views in turn suggest different ways to measure quality. At the extreme, the prescriptive view would seek 'objective' evidence of individual functioning, the 'free market' view would concentrate on user satisfaction, and the social change view would look at the degree of inclusion and participation by users in society.

Some examples

P.A.S.S. (Wolfensberger and Glenn, 1975) was one of the first attempts to codify quality in human services in relation to a specific set of values – in this case, the principle of normalization. It identifies 50 domains to define the quality of the service, covering for example the building, management staff qualities, and links to ordinary resources. O'Brien and Lyle (1988) suggested five major accomplishments for human services – sharing ordinary places, making choices, developing competencies, being treated with respect and having a valued social role, and growing in personal relationships. More recently, the Social Services Inspectorate (1990) has popularized six key outcomes for residential services – dignity, choice, fulfilment, independence, rights, and privacy. It should be noted that there is often potential conflict between outcomes: should a service encourage someone to stay with a lifetime friend or to move to a less restricted setting, to wear purple or to go for grey?

Who does the defining?

In any particular service, a variety of processes shape the definition of quality: custom and practice, requirements of the local authority or the legislative framework, expressed expectations of users, operational policies, the service-level agreement with the purchaser, and values imported by new staff.

157

Clarity and ownership in the definition of quality are essential. A good quality assurance process brings staff and users in to the process of defining and redefining quality. It does this, however, within the overall set of values that defines the agency. The trick is to create local frameworks that allow diversity and ownership while providing guidance and boundaries.

Assessing performance

Assessment can be internal, collaborative or external, it can be continuous or periodic, and it can be oriented towards detail or towards pattern. It is about *collating evidence* from a number of sources and *forming judgments* about the connections between philosophy, practice, resoures and outcomes.

Internal, collaborative or external

Much of the responsibility for assessing performance rests with the programme staff and manager. Is the building safe? Do people get the support agreed at the time agreed? Are the staff competent? How often are people able to get out? Has anyone made any new friends? How much are people earning? Do we contribute to a positive public image for our clients? Asking and answering these sorts of questions should be built in to the recording and supervision systems in the service.

If a standard has been agreed that each resident has the opportunity to go out individually with support at least once a week, the keyworking system should be able to yield that information and to take action if people are being failed by the service.

At the same time, there are benefits in 'new eyes' – whether an inspector, a hired consultant, a manager from another unit or a users' organization. This applies particularly to 'picking up' interactions between staff and user, seeing how the building really looks to an outsider, and seeing the wood for the trees. People immersed in a service can find it hard to see patterns – for example, staff being rushed off their feet while users have nothing to do.

External assessments – whether long-term evaluations or unannounced visits by inspectors – have their place, but unless programme staff understand and accept the views of the external assessor, voluntary change is unlikely.

Continuous or periodic

Continuous assessment mechanisms allow for continuous adjustment of performance. The recording system has to be designed to yield information relevant to quality assurance – for example, how people spend their day in a day centre may be recorded in a standard format once per week by the user with staff assistance, punctuality or customer satisfaction may be recorded at each visit by the home care assistant and confirmed by the customer, the time between a referral and a response by the service may be logged by the administrator. The amount of information that could be collected is infinite. Care must be taken to collect the most relevant information and to ensure that there is time for someone to analyze and act on it. There may be opportunity in large organizations to reshape the information already sought routinely, so that these returns become more quality relevant.

Positive monitoring by peers or by the line manager provides another way to assess quality on a continuous basis. This can be highly systematic – every tenth visit is accompanied and a feedback sheet completed by a colleague – or quite informal. Either way it can help staff think about what they are doing – the most basic ingredient in quality assurance.

Quality circles and **quality action groups** bring stakeholders together on a continuous basis to discuss quality, identify shortfalls and initiate change. They are likely to collect additional information that relates to a specific problem under investigation. Again, they will be more effective if the routine information collected is robust and relevant.

There is also value in periodic assessments, taking a good look at everything the service does. This helps to create a cycle that then supports the continuous processes, encourages a sense of seriousness and allows time to ask new questions. This periodic assessment may be the focus for involving outsiders such as inspectors.

Details or pattern

The assessment process can go into enormous detail or rely on metaphor and impression. Too much detail can lock a service into an emphasis on the easily countable at the expense of the important. A day centre could know exactly how many sessions started more than five minutes late in the last year and how many people attended each one, but fail to see that most of the people are bored for most of the time.

It is important to link the detailed evidence to the 'theory in use' of the service, as it is that theory in use that may need to change or at least to be made explicit before major change can happen. On the other hand, impressionistic judgments may fail to give any clues about what to build on in the short to medium term.

There are key sources of evidence: the look and feel of the service, the image it puts out through publicity materials, what actually happens in service transactions, the management mechanisms, and the judgments of staff, carers, other agencies and users.

The most important source of evidence is the users. Their satisfaction with the service is an important indicator, though not the only one. The impact of the service on their day-to-day lives (has it been effective?) is also important. Users may express satisfaction with a service that is friendly even if it is ineffective or even counterproductive. In a residential setting they are usually the only people present 24 hours a day, 7 days a week and therefore have a wealth of information. Many will have used other services with which to compare this one – this gives an important insight and perspective. For this reason, a good quality assurance system goes hand in hand with a good system of care planning and effective methods of user participation.

For both internal and external assessors, spending time with one or more users may be an important element in the process. This 'being with' is very different from 'working with' or 'interviewing' the users, and while it may not generate the same detailed evidence, it may give a better insight into what life is like for a user in this service and which concerns are most critical.

Making changes to improve performance

If the service is serious about improving quality, and if this seriousness is shared by the purchaser and/or by line management, then significant change is usually possible, even without a major increase in direct resources. In the absence of such seriousness, the pretence of change can go on for a long time and itself contribute to low morale and poor practice.

For units where change is possible, there are two key issues: firstly, involving the stakeholders (including the users and external agencies) in the change and, secondly, seeing change not as a linear process at the end of which things will be okay, but as a continuous process of adjustment and feedback that will itself influence the unit's definition of quality.

A quality assurance system will not make major change happen in an organization that does not want to change. If it is to be effective it has to be built-in to management, not bolted-on, and so will broadly reflect the current culture and values. A quality assurance system will not fix or cure incompetent managers: it is not for the quality assurance system to tell senior managers what they already know or to put the boot in on their behalf.

A quality assurance system *may* make it more likely that an agency gets a contract: the rush to BS5750 is motivated in part by the desire for an externally recognized seal of approval, even though it says nothing about the quality of the service, only about its quality assurance system.

A good quality assurance system has the following features: it is cyclical, it is explicit and understood by staff, it is participative and geared towards improvement rather than blaming, it is based on a definition of quality that has been agreed with users, it allows for flexibility in the way it operates at a local level, it is subject to planned review and change, it has the commitment of senior managers in the organization, it respects users' privacy, it is sophisticated enough for the organization's current stage of development without overloading other systems, and it is fun (at least sometimes).

A good quality assurance system will encourage a culture of reflection and dialogue, provide guidance, feedback and motivation for staff, and generate continuous if gradual improvement in the quality of the service, other things being equal. It will allow the service to offer a clearer contract to users and to purchasers, and to market itself more effectively. It will cost time and therefore money; some of this will be time already spent in supervision or problem-solving by middle managers. It will save time by increasing the clarity of staff roles and by focusing the service more closely on agreed outcomes.

The process of quality assurance, if designed and implemented in a way that engages staff and users, can be empowering and energizing. It does, however, demand a reciprocal commitment from senior managers.

17 *The art of inspection* *Joan Culberson Beck*

The development of inspection units within departments of social services and social work is a requirement of the National Health Service and Community Care Act (1990). Inspection units were to be implemented by 1 April 1991, not as an end in themselves, but as part of the phased implementation of the Act. On that date departments of social services and social work were required to set up inspection units to inspect and report on both local authority provision and registerable independent residential homes.

The development of inspection

The idea of inspection within the personal social services is not new. The duty to register and inspect a variety of residential provision is clearly set out in the Registered Homes Act (1984). Since 1984 registration and inspection has been required of residential homes for older people, the physically disabled, people with learning difficulties and those with mental ill health within the private and voluntary sector, commonly put together and called the independent sector.

Between 1984 and 1991 local authorities developed expectations for those homes in the independent sector, but concern was expressed by a variety of bodies that separate expectations could be required of provision in this sector. Attention was continually drawn to the fact that whilst the local authority inspected residential care in the independent sector, local authority provision did not receive the same systematic assessment and appraisal by either its own staff or an independent body. The development of inspection units and the requirement for

162

local authority provision to be inspected to the same standards as those expected of the independent sector has been welcomed by many, but has generated speculation about just what the inspectors will find. The requirement for independent inspection units to apply the same standards to all residential care, including local authority care, was recommended by the Wagner Report in 1988.

The Department of Health guidance on inspection units, *Inspecting for Quality* (HMSO, 1991) makes several recommendations about the development of inspection units, among them:

- independence of the units should be ensured through the autonomy of the head of unit, who should be a senior manager
- unit procedures should be grounded on well-established principles of inspection and reports should be open to the public
- standards should be developed through participatory means
- advisory committees should be established
- units should be comprised of staff with an appropriate range of specialist skills.

It is important to note that no matter what the eventual workload of any one inspection unit might be, at the moment the statutory responsibility to inspect is for residential care only, although the Children Act 1989 does give local authorities the duty to register and inspect day care provision for children under eight. Reasons for the focus on residential care are threefold: firstly, as a response to scandals and an attempt to regain the public's confidence in residential care, secondly, as a genuine desire to ensure quality standards are available to some of the most dependent and vulnerable people in society, and lastly to ensure value for taxpayers' money as residential care costs continue to rise.

It is unfortunate that the opportunity was missed for making a legislative requirement for the providers of domiciliary care and day care to be brought into the registration and inspection umbrella.

The statutory requirement to establish inspection units has not resulted in any national uniformity. Guidance from the DOH has been interpreted by local authorities in the light of local politics, existing personnel, and individual social services committees' views. Inspection units have been developed as quality assurance units, consumer affairs units and jointly with health authorities.

The heads of units have been appointed at senior, principal and chief officer levels, and the number of homes on any one inspector's

163

workload ranges from 10 to 80. Some units deal only with residential care for adults, but most have responsibilities for children's establishments as well, and some have had other responsibilities added on. Most frequent of these 'extra' duties is the oversight of the complaints procedure. Still others have been developed with the remit to inspect all services provided by the social services department. As a result, there are probably as many permutations of inspection units as there are local authorities.

The use of the term quality assurance is not strictly speaking descriptive of the work of most inspection units. Quality assurance is about being sure that all aspects of a service are right: the plan, the staff hours, the training of staff, the administrative support, the shops that provide the food, etc. Quality assurance is everyone's job. The job of inspection units is quality control, taking a snapshot of an aspect of a service and evaluating it, much as the quality control people in a bakery taste one in every 1,000 loaves of bread. Inspectors sample a minimum of two days' life in the residential home. The two or ten day experience of inspectors does not imply that they know what it would be like to live in any one particular home, let alone what it is like for people of a different age, race or gender. This is information that only the residents know and this knowledge will vary from one resident to another, based on their own individual experiences and perceptions.

It would be wrong, however, to think of the role of the inspector in terms of the two statutory inspections per year required by the legislation. It is better to think in terms of an annual cycle of inspection, which includes statutory inspections, one announced and one unannounced, and the investigation of complaints. Any unannounced visits to the home, indeed any contact with the home, forms part of the cycle of inspection. It is important to remember that there is no concept of 'informal' in inspection, all contact with the establishment, its staff, owner, residents or relatives provides insight into the quality of life of residents.

The art and science of inspection

Having said that neither the idea of inspection units nor the role of inspector is new, there is still considerable scope for development of the tasks and skills involved. Many inspectors of independent homes before 1991 worked in environments with very little understanding of their task, little support, and sometimes in atmospheres of mistrust and hostility towards the independent sector, particularly the private sector. Some of the areas for development include the use of positive indicators for some of the less tangible, less quantifiable parts of inspection, enabling residents to give an honest view of their life in the home, the involvement of informal regulators in the inspection task, public access to inspection reports, training of inspectors, the possibility of national standards, and the quality control aspects of all service delivery, not just residential care.

All of these developments are what I would call the art of inspection. The science of inspection, the measuring of rooms, the inspection of records, the checking of the visual appearance of the home, is the easier part of inspection and sadly is all that some inspectors have time for. The art of inspecting is that of judging the likely quality of life, the experience of living in the home, and the quality of interactions. The art of inspection is less easy, less quantifiable and more open to individual interpretation.

As inspectors we must begin to identify positive indicators to the quality of the less tangible areas of people's life such as those areas highlighted in *Homes Are For Living In* (HMSO, 1989) privacy, dignity, independence, choice, rights, and fulfilment. These less tangible elements of inspection require that the inspector considers what underlies the apparently objective facts. This is where the objectivity of inspection is aided by the process of thinking and acting that is the art of inspection. As an illustration of the art of inspection in all six of these areas consider breakfast, more importantly, breakfast in bed.

Many managers of homes will tell you proudly that all their residents have breakfast in bed. To some people this is the ultimate luxury and one they think their older relative or client is entitled to in their advancing years. Questions to ask yourself about this include what choice do residents have, can they have their breakfast in the dining room if they like? How does the home ascertain what the resident wishes to have for breakfast on any given morning, and what time they would like it? Juggling a cup and saucer, pot of tea and boiled egg on one's lap is difficult even for those at the peak of their physical fitness, what of those with arthritis or cataracts? Where is the dignity in breakfast in bed for those with nocturnal continence problems? Frequently older people find that they need less sleep than they did when they were young, that despite any aches and pains they may have when they wake up they feel better once they get up and dressed, that the provision of meals in residential care is something to be looked forward to. What consideration has there been to these issues? How do residents know the answers?

In considering the art of inspection ask yourself what you notice when walking into a resident's room? Has the resident been involved in the decoration and furnishing of the room, does it reflect their own personality or the personality of the manager? Does what you see confirm a high value on the people who live in the home? Does the choice of pictures and ornaments reflect the values of residents or does it devalue other residents? For example, the overabundance of Christian decorations may make some people feel uncomfortable, as would a picture depicting black people as slaves.

The art of inspection is about seeing or hearing one thing and being able to form a view of another, and then testing the information. On entering a large residential home you encounter an open hallway with comfortable chairs, plants, and people in small groups talking. This might be an indication that this is a home that welcomes and encourages visitors. On the other hand this might also be a home that affords no privacy to residents receiving visitors and likes to keep them together to ensure that they are supervised. What assumption will you make, and how will you test your assumption?

There are several areas for development of the art of inspection, what follows is an explanation of those that can provide a useful start and that I consider to be most important.

Seeking residents' views

The inability of inspectors to know what it is like to live in a home places a high value on service user participation in inspections. In my opinion the ability to listen is one of the inspectors most necessary and under-rated skills. The time to listen should also be the privilege of inspection as no inspection is complete without the recording of the views of the people who actually live in the home. This is easier said than done and the inspector will have to develop a repertoire of ways to encourage and enable residents to comment on the care they receive and to explain their perception of their life. Inspectors will also need to know how to listen between the lines, for example many residents when asked what they think of the staff will respond with 'they're very busy here', or 'the others need much more attention than I do'. These responses tell us about the lack of interaction residents have with care staff as they see them running from one task to another with little time for personal attention.

Comments such as those above also give the inspector insight into how legitimate the resident feels their requests are. Explicit standards, however exemplary they may be, can be undermined by the process and delivery of care. The possiblity of non-task-centred interaction with residents may not be a part of the ethos of the home. This will be evident by the interactions between residents and staff, particularly when conversations all centre around physical requirements and residents have long since learned not to ask for the less tangible – the smile, the quiet chat, the joke, or the insight into staff's life outside the home. Food and the provision of meals is an important aspect of residential care. Residents tell us a lot with comments like 'it's not like home', 'can't complain' or 'well, they try hard'. What is not said is sometimes more important than what is said.

Many residents will have communication difficulties and the onus is on the inspector to try to get over those. A vast area for development is in the involvement of elderly mentally infirm people in the inspection process and we must remember that a resident telling us at eight o'clock at night that they have not eaten since yesterday may not remember the three meals they have had in the intervening period. What the inspector remembers from these interactions is how they are dealt with by the staff and what lead the staff get from their managers.

The discussion of enabling residents to speak freely to inspectors raises the importance of the inspector being a regular and welcome visitor to the home, not one who visits the statutory twice a year and spends most of the time with the staff.

Informal regulators

There are a great many people who go in and out of a residential care home but have no statutory part to play in inspection. Ways of seeking these people's views and enabling them to contribute to the cycle of inspection is a vital area for development. Such informal regulators include relatives, volunteers, clergy and the people who deliver the milk, papers and groceries. The views of the neighbours are important, as is the view of the person who drives the mobile library. I have a colleague who maintains his father was an expert on the quality of residential care provided in the town where he grew up: his father was the local greengrocer and was able to form a view of the homes based on the variety and quantity of the weekly order and the willingness, or lack of willingness, of the home to accept poor quality produce.

Those in the independent sector will be well aware, and local authority managers would be wise to remember, that the best advert for a service is not a glossy brochure, but word of mouth and neighbours' recommendations.

Access to inspection reports

The public access to inspection reports is a recommendation within the guidance given by the Department of Health. How this is done and, indeed, whether it is done, will vary from unit to unit. Some units have implemented an extremely open approach, including the availability of inspection reports at local libraries; others have more restricted access, with reports available to existing and potential residents and their relatives only. Still other units have decided that the public accessibility of the inspection report is a matter for the individual home owner only.

Some national consensus on the access to reports would not only be useful to the staff in inspection units, but to users, relatives and friends trying to assess the merits of different homes. A national review of access would not only inform practice but might lead to more publicity about the procedures and to more public use of them.

Inspecting services other than residential care

I have already said that some units have been developed with a department-wide brief rather than being restricted to residential care only. I have also mentioned the fact that the government of the day did not see fit to include domiciliary care and day care in the registration requirement. The setting of standards and inspection of services other than residential care is one of the major challenges facing inspection units. Residential care has long been seen as one of the Cinderella services and the requirement to inspect only residential care does little to dispel that myth. We have all seen the shortfalls in a variety of service delivery within departments of social work and social services. If departments truly intend offering quality service to their service users they will have to monitor *all* their services, at least at arms length, paying due regard to the outcomes of that monitoring and make changes.

For very many years residential care and the staff who work within it had to learn from the work of their colleagues in other parts of social care services: on training courses they have had to transfer the case work examples given into group care, they have read the theory of individual work and generalized into group living, they have looked at the attention and all too frequently the resources going into child care. We now have a perfect opportunity for the other parts of the service to learn lessons from the experience of the residential sector. In the last two years, residential care has been highlighted not only by the press, but by the academics, the DOH and our own departments. This is an opportunity to be seized.

Conclusion

The past couple of years have seen tremendous developments in the inspection process and the setting up of inspection units. It sometimes seems that every government suggestion gives more responsibility to inspection units. It must be remembered that the statutory work comes first, no matter how enticing some of the new suggestions are. We must ensure that inspection units are adequately resourced to enable the inspection process and the necessary developments of the art of inspection or it will be only the service user who loses, again.

Unless we spend the time developing the art of inspection we will be like the 'inspectors' of my youth who checked whether the lake was safe to skate on. They knew the depth of the ice, the temperature of the ice, and identified evident cracks; they knew nothing of the clarity of the water and the existence of the life beneath the ice. Residents in residential homes not only desire to skate on the ice, but to sink or swim in the unplumbed depths below.

Whether independent inspection units work or not will be dependent on the receptiveness of organizations, the attitude of officers, and the diplomatic skills of the heads of units. The success of units should not be judged by how hard hitting their reports are, how many homes they close or by how popular they are with directors of social services, but by the impact they are able to make on improving the quality of the daily life of the individuals who live in residential homes and by their influence in the setting of quality standards for all service users in a way that is genuinely independent of vested interests.

Conclusion: *Likely impossibility or unconvincing possibility?*

As well as telling us that 'man is by nature a political animal', Aristotle is reported as saying that 'a likely impossibility is always preferable to an unconvincing possibility'. In which of these terms should we view the future of community care?

The origins of the present community care legislation lay in the recognition by government of the imminent impossibility, in financial terms, of providing care for the dramatically increasing numbers of elderly people in the ways that were currently in use. In particular, the restrictions of 'the perverse incentive' prevented non-residential care options being used to diminish the escalating costs for Social Security of private residential care. The purpose of transferring funds from Social Security to local authority social services/work departments was to create the freedom for innovative and flexible forms of care provision in the community. Yet the chance that this will ensure a good care service for the users of community care services seems to many people to be an unconvincing possibility.

Although 'the greater part of care has been, is and always will be provided by families and friends', does this mean that placing the onus on family, and particularly female relatives, to provide even more care will result in the provision of a good quality of life for dependent people who are elderly, infirm or disabled and for their carers? On the face of it, this seems an unconvincing possibility for a number of reasons. Firstly, those needing the care can need substantial and increasing amounts of it, as in the case of Alzheimers disease. Secondly, the potential carers in the family will often already have many other caring responsibilities, e.g. to partners or children, and the welfare of these people and the quality of relationships with them can be seriously

171

jeopardised by the tensions, practical difficulties and emotional strains of taking on a demanding additional commitment. Thirdly, in the present financial context many families in which there are two partners require both of them to be earning in order to meet their essential living costs and the loss of a wage to take on the care of a relative may simply be impossible. Extensive loss of earnings at this stage also carries a penalty in terms of pension entitlement. Finally, the shift in family patterns, with a much higher incidence of people who are divorced, single parents or in reconstituted families, may also mean that for an increasing number of people it will genuinely be impossible to take on the additional demands of providing care, for indefinite periods, to dependent friends or relatives.

For people willing to take on the role of carer, the task will often be a daunting one and they will need to be assisted by the provision of good levels of practical, emotional and financial support. The lack of such provision will simply lead to a breakdown in the care arrangements. Evidence of this can already be seen in instances of elderly people abandoned by their exhausted carers in hospital, day care centres or at the end of periods of respite care. Yet providing good levels of support for community carers will not be a cheap option and will therefore place a real strain on the budgets local authorities have available for this purpose.

The potential exists in the new community care legislation for a pattern of high quality services to develop, which are based on a careful assessment of individual service users' needs, wishes and circumstances and tailored to fit these. What may make this optimistic scenario seem to many people to be an unconvincing possibility or an impossibility is the belief that the government's present commitment to cutting public expenditure will result in a totally inadequate level of funding for these developments. If this happens, the careful attention given to the assessment of the needs and circumstances of individual service users will no longer be used primarily as the creative determinant of individually tailored packages of care but will become the criterion of rationing the inadequate supply of services.

What might, however, turn the apparent impossibility of the more optimistic scenario described above into a likely impossibility is the new power given to the voice of the consumer. The legal requirement placed on the service providers to ascertain the wishes of service users, in order to build appropriate, individually tailored packages of care, will raise high levels of expectation in service users and their social networks. If these expectations are frustrated and service users choose to exert their power as consumers and monitors of the service, and also as the electors of the politicians who are ultimately accountable for the services, then the potential of community care could become a reality. As people who are vulnerable through age, disability or infirmity, plus their relatives, form an increasing proportion of the electorate, so their ability to put concerted pressure on the government increases. The power to influence through the ballot box has been seen in America in organisations such as the Gray Panther Movement and has led to some significant outcomes. Perhaps as optimists we should hope that the increasing scale and the centrality of the consumer groups in community care will turn the present unconvincing possibility of a truly creative and well resourced system of community care into a more likely impossibility.

References

Chapter 1

Audit Department, *Making a Reality of Community Care*, HMSO, 1986.
BANK-MIKKELSON, N.E., 'A Metropolitan area in Denmark', in KUGEL, R. and WOLFENSBERGER, W., ed., *Changing Patterns in Residential Services for the Mentally Retarded*, President's Commission on Mental Retardation, Washington, 1969.
BEEFORTH, M., et al., *Whose service is it anyway?*, London, Research and Development for Psychiatry, 1990.
Department of Health, *Caring for People: Community Care in the Next Decade and Beyond*, Cmnd 849, HMSO, 1989.
Department of Health, *Purchase of Service: Practice Guidance*, HMSO, 1991.
ENNIS, E., et al., *Planning and Managing Community Care (Part 3)*, University of Dundee, 1991.
FIEDLER, B., *Living Options Lottery – Report on Living Options Project*, Prince of Wales Advisory Commission on Disability, 1988.
FREIRE, P., *Cultural Action for Freedom*, Penguin, London, 1972.
GRIFFITHS, SIR R., *Community Care: Agenda for Action*, HMSO, 1988.
HANDY, C., *The Age of Unreason*, Arrow Books, London, 1989.
HOGGETT, P., *Modernisation, Political Strategy and the Welfare State: An Organisational Perspective*, School of Advanced Urban Studies, Bristol, 1990.
ILLICH, I., *Medical Nemesis*, Calder amd Boyars, 1975.
MURRAY, F., 'The decentralisation of production: the decline of the mass collective', *Capital and Class*, no.19, 1983.
McEWEN, E., ed., *Age: the Unrecognised Discrimination*, Age Concern, London, 1990.
McKNIGHT, J., in MOUNT, B., and ZWERNIK, K., *It's Never Too Early, It's Never Too Late – a Booklet about Personal Futures Planning*, Minnesota Metropolitan Council, undated.
PERSKE, R., and PERSKE, M., *Circles of Friends*, Abingdon Press, Nashville, 1988.
PIRIE, M., and BUTLER, E., *Extending Care*, Adam Smith Institute, London, 1989.

O'BRIEN, J., and LYLE, C., *Framework for Accomplishment*, Responsive System Associates, Georgia, 1988.

OLIVER, M., *The Politics of Disablement*, Macmillan, Basingstoke, 1990.

SNOW, J., *The Role of Disability in Shaping Responsive Community*, Centre for Integrated Education and Community, Toronto, 1987.

WISTOW, G., *Community Care Planning: A Review of Past and Future Imperatives, Caring for People Implementation Document CC14*, HMSO, 1990.

WOLFENSBERGER, W., 'Social role valorisation: a proposed new term for the principle of normalisation' in *Mental Retardation*, vol. 21, no. 6, 1983, pp. 234–9.

WOLFENSBERGER, W., *The History and Nature of Our Institutional Models*, New York Center on Human Policy, Syracuse, 1975.

Chapter 2

The original draft of this chapter contained 2,000 words in references, these have been replaced by the two literature reviews referred to below:

SINCLAIR, I.A.C., 'Residential care for elderly people', in SINCLAIR, I.A.C., ed., *Residential Care: The Research Reviewed. Literature Surveys Commissioned by the Independent Review of Residential Care*, HMSO, 1988.

SINCLAIR, I.A.C., et al., *The Kaleidoscope of Care: A Review of Research on Welfare Provision for Elderly People*, HMSO, 1990.

Chapter 3

Association of Directors of Social Work, Adults at Risk – Draft Discussion, June 1990.

ARONSON, M.K., ed., *The Acting-Out Elderly*, Haworth, New York.

Department of Health, *Caring for People: Community Care in the Next Decade and Beyond*, Cmnd 849, HMSO, 1989.

Disabled Persons *(Services, Consultation and Representation) Act*, HMSO, 1986.

English and Welsh Law Commission, *Mentally Incapacitated Adults and Decision-Making*, Consultation Paper 119, HMSO, 1991.

EVANDROU, M., *Challenging the Invisibility of Carers: Mapping Informal Care Nationally*, LSE, London, 1990.

JACQUES, A., *Understanding Dementia*, Churchill Livingstone, 1988.

McCREADIE, R., *Dementia and the Law: The Challenge Ahead*, Scottish Action on Dementia, Edinburgh, 1989.

McLAUGHLIN, P., *Guardianship of the Person*, National Institute on Mental Retardation, Toronto, 1977.

National Schizophrenia Fellowship, *Short Report – Short Change*, Kingston, London, 1986.

NICHOLS, D.I., Seminar Paper, unpublished, Department of Social Policy and Social Work, Edinburgh University, 1991.

PERSKE, R., 'Dignity of risk', in WOLFENSBERGER (1972).

PETERS, D., *A Better Life*, Scottish Home and Health Department/Scottish Education Department, 1979.

SAMUEL, E., et al., *Process and Preference: Assessment of Older People for Institutional Care*, Central Research Unit, Scottish Office, forthcoming.

Scottish Law Commission, *Mentally Disabled Adults: Legal Arrangements for Managing their Welfare and Finances, Discussion Paper 94*, HMSO, Edinburgh, 1991.

WHYTE, B., and HUNTER, S., 'Guardianship of the person in Scotland', *British Journal of Social Work*, vol. 22, no. 2, pp. 167–86, 1992.

WHYTE, B., and HUNTER, S., *Mental Health Officers and Guardianship of the Person*, unpublished report, Edinburgh University, 1989.

WOLFENSBERGER, W., *The Principles of Normalization in Human Services*, National Institute on Mental Retardation, Toronto, 1972.

Chapter 4

ATKIN, K., 'Community care in a multi-racial society: incorporating the user view', *Policy and Politics*, Vol. 19, no. 3, July 1991, pp. 159–67.

ATKIN, K., CAMERON, E., BADGER, F., and EVERS, H., 'Asian elders' knowledge and future use of community social and health services', *New Community* 15(3), 1989.

BHALLA, A., and BLAKEMORE, K., *Elders of the Minority Ethnic Groups (Birmingham Survey)* AFFOR, 1987.

BIGGS, S., 'Consumers, case management and inspection: obscuring social deprivation and need?', *Critical Social Policy*, no. 30, 1990.

BLAKEMORE, K., 'The state, the voluntary sector and new developments in provision for old of minority racial groups', *Ageing and Society* 5, 1985.

BOWLING, B., *Elderly People from Ethnic Minorities: A Report on Four Projects*, ACIOG, 1990.

BURDETT, J., *Contracts, Paper given at Black Policy Advisers Seminar, Organisation Development Unit*, NCVO, 24 April 1990.

BUTT, J., 'More than just record keeping?' *Share Newsletter*, Issue 2, March 1992 (research is entitled 'Equally Fair?'), NISW, London.

CHAUHAN, K., 'Asian groups call for consultation', *Disability Issues*, No. 4, p. 3, February/March 1992.

DAURADO, P., 'Getting the message across', *Community Care*, 21 March 1991.

DUTT, R., *Interview with Ratna Dutt: Black Communities Care: Information about your Rights*, NISW, Leeds, 1991, pp. 12–13.

FRANCIS, E., *Mental Health, Antiracism and Social Work Training in One Small Step Towards Racial Justice*, CCETSW, 1991, pp. 81–96.

MIRZA, K., *Community Care for the Black Community in One Small Step Towards Racial Justice*, CCETSW, 1991, pp. 120–47.

MISHAN, E.J., *Consumer Choice Rules the Market: Twenty-one Popular Economic Fallacies*, Pelican, 1971.

MOORE, W., 'Older Asians lose out in Harrow', *Social Work Today*, 31 October 1991.

NORMAN, A., *Triple Jeopardy: Growing Old in a Second Homeland*, Centre for Policy on Ageing, 1985.

PATEL, N., Do we Need Rational Choice Theory? Unpublished paper, 1989.

PATEL, N., *A 'Race' Against Time? Social Services Provision to Black Elders*, The Runnymede Trust, 1990.

PFEFFER, K., and COOTE, A., *Is Quality Good for You? A Critical Review of Quality Assurance in Welfare Services*, Social Policy Paper No.5, IPPR, 1991.

PHAROAH, C., and REDMON, E., 'Care for ethnic elders', *The Health Service Journal*, 16 May 1991.

PHILLIPSON, C., *Delivering community care services for older people: problems and prospects for the 1990'*, Centre for Social Gerontology, Working Paper No.3, University of Keele, 1990.

Runnymede Trust and Radical Statistics Group, *Britain's Black Population*, Heinemann Educational Books, 1980.

SIVANANDAN, A., 'Black struggles against racism', Setting the Context for Change, *Anti-Racist Social Work Education Series*, no. 1, CCETSW, 1991.

Footnotes:

1. Phillipson, C. (1990) in his critique raises some important questions on this and suggests that community care should have also been about 'what' and 'how'.
2. For a fuller explanation see Patel (Chapters 4 and 5, 1990).
3. Despite the increase in £28 billion PSBR in 1992.
4. Particularly since their concentration is likely to reflect the fact that '80% of black people are concentrated in just 10% of the census numeration districts'.
5. I am not by any means suggesting that a large black agency provider will always be progressive and non-oppressive.
6. Anecdotal evidence from many day centre co-ordinators suggests that creative active development of services are blighted and the focus continues to be on *parity* of services with white groups – in other words black elders are 'inserted' using services for white elders as *base*, with some modifications, which are necessary but not sufficient.
7. Since writing this chapter, several interesting and relevant items have been published and/or are forthcoming. These include:
   (a) Newham Black and Ethnic Minority Community Care Forum Report, 'Community Care: The Newham Black Experience', December 1992 (available from 19 Carlton Road, London E12 5BG).
   (b) London Group on Race Aspects of Community Care (1992) 'Black Communities: Who Cares?'
   (c) National Association of Race Equality Advisers (1993) 'Black Community Care Charter' (available from Race Relations Unit, Congreve House, 3 Congreve Passage, Birmingham B3 3DA).
   (d) A collection of papers (forthcoming from CCETSW) on Black Communities and Community Care (J. Bourne); Case Management Models and Anti-racism (F. Bartels).

Chapter 5

Audit Commission, *The Reality of Community Care*, HMSO, 1986.

CHALLIS, L., FULLER, S., HENWOOD, M., KLEIN, R., PLOWDEN, W., WEBB,

A., WHITTINGHAM, P., and WISTOW, G., *Joint Approaches to Social Policy: Rationality and Practice*, Cambridge University Press, Cambridge, 1988.

Department of Health, *Community Care in the Next Decade and Beyond: Policy Guidance*, HMSO, 1990.

Department of Health etc., Care Management and Assessment: Managers' Guide, HMSO, 1991.

GLENNERSTER, H., KORMAN, N., and MARSLEN-WILSON, F., *Planning for Priority Groups*, Martin Robertson, Oxford, 1983.

GRIFFITHS, SIR R., *Community Care: Agenda for Action*, HMSO, 1988.

House of Commons etc., *26th Report, Session 1987/88*, HMSO, 1988.

House of Commons etc., *Community Care: Planning and Co-operation*, Eighth Report, Session 1989–90, HMSO, 1990.

HUNTER, D.J., and RICHARDS, H., *Towards a Framework for Joint Planning in Scotland*, Central Research Unit Paper, Scottish Office, Edinburgh, 1990.

HUNTER, D.J., and WISTOW, G., *Community Care in Britain: Variations on a Theme*, King Edward's Hospital Fund for London, London, 1987.

HUNTER, D.J., and WISTOW, G., *Elderly People's Integrated Care System (EPICS): An Organisational, Policy and Practice Review*, Nuffield Institute Reports No.3, Nuffield Institute for Services Studies, Leeds, 1991.

WISTOW, G., and HARDY, B., 'Joint Management in Community Care', *Journal of Management in Medicine* 5, no. 4, 1991, pp. 40–48.

Working Group on Joint Planning, *Progress in Partnership*, Department of Health and Social Security, London, 1985.

Chapter 6

COSLA, *Implementation of Community Care in Scotland*, 1991.

Department of Health, *Caring for People: Community Care in the Next Decade and Beyond*, HMSO, 1989.

Department of Health for Scotland, *The Housing of Special Groups*, HMSO, 1952.

GIBB, M., and MUNRO, K., *Housing Finance in the UK*, Macmillan, 1991.

GREVE, J., and CURRIE, E., *Homelessness in Britain*, Joseph Rowntree Memorial Trust, 1990.

GRIFFITHS, SIR R., *Community Care: Agenda for Action*, HMSO, 1988.

KOHLS, M., *Stop, Start, Stutter*, Care in the Community Scottish Working Group, 1989.

Joint Health and Social Services Board, *People First, Northern Ireland*, HMSO, 1990.

LOWE, S., and HUGHES, D., eds., *A New Century of Social Housing*, London University Press, 1992.

Morris Report, *Housing and Social Work – A Joint Approach*, Scottish Development Department, HMSO, Edinburgh, 1975.

National Federation of Housing Associations, *Housing – the Foundation of Community Care*, 1989.

Scottish Home and Health Department, *Joint Planning and Support Finance Circular*, Scottish Office, 1985.

Scottish Home and Health Department, *Scottish Health Priorities into the Eighties (SHAPE)*, HMSO, Edinburgh, 1981.
WAGNER, G., *Residential Care – A Positive Choice*, NISW, 1988.

Chapter 7

Consumer Involvement Sub-Group, All Wales Advisory Panel, *Consumer Involvement and the All Wales Strategy*, Welsh Office Information Division, 1991.
Department of Health, *Community Care in the Next Decade and Beyond: Policy Guidance*, HMSO, 1989.
LEAT, D., *Voluntary Organisations and Accountability*, Policy Analysis Unit, NCVO, 1988.
McGRATH, M., 'Consumer participation in service planning – the AWS experience', *Journal of Social policy* 18, no. 19, 1989, pp. 67–89.
National Health Service and Community Care Act 1990, HMSO, 1990.
OSBORN, A., *Taking Part in Community Care Planning. The Involvement of User Groups, Carer Groups and Voluntary Groups*, Nuffield Institute for Health Services Studies and Age Concern Scotland, 1991.
Scottish Education Department/Scottish Home and Health Department, *Community Care in Scotland, Community Care Planning*, Scottish Office, 1991 (SW1/1991 SHHD.DMG (1991)1)
Welsh Consumer Council, *Putting People First: Consumer Consultation and Community Care*, Cardiff – Welsh Consumer Council, November 1990.
Welsh Office, *Guidance on Social Care Plans*, Welsh Office, September 1990.

Chapter 8

Audit Commission, *Making a Reality of Community Care*, HMSO, 1986.
GRIFFITHS, SIR R., *Community Care: An Agenda for Action*, HMSO, 1988.

Chapter 9

BACHRACH, L., 'Overview: Model Programs for Chronic Mental Patients' *American Journal of Psychiatry*, 137:9, 1980, pp. 1023–31.
BEECHAM, J., KNAPP, M., and FENYO, A., 'Costs, Needs and Outcomes', *Schizophrenia Bulletin*, vol.17, no.3, pp. 427–39.
BEEFORTH, M., et al., *Whose Service is it Anyway?* Research and Development for Psychiatry, 1990.
DEAN, C., and GADD, E. 'An inner city home treatment service for acute psychiatric patients', *Psychiatric Bulletin*, No. 13, 1989, pp. 667–9.
Department of Health, *Community Care in the Next Decade and Beyond: Policy Guidance*, HMSO, 1989.
Department of Health and Social Security, *Better Services for the Mentally Ill*, HMSO, 1975.
FALLOON, I., et al., 'Developing family-based care for schizophrenia: a training project', *Psychiatric Bulletin*, No. 13, 1989, pp. 675–6.

HOGMAN, G., and WESTALL, J., *The Mental Illness Specific Grant, the Early Days*, National Schizophrenia Fellowship, 1991.

JOSEPH, P., 'Mentally disordered homeless offenders – diversion from custody', *Health Trends*, vol. 22, no. 2, 1990, pp. 51–3.

KNAPP, M., et al., *Care in the Community: Evaluating a Demonstration Programme*, Gower, 1991.

Lambeth Link, *Community Self Assessment Form*, Lambeth Link, 1991.

MARKS, I., CONNOLLY,J and MUIJEN, M., 'The Maudsley Daily Living Programme', *Bulletin of the Royal College of Psychiatrists*, No. 12, 1988, pp. 22–4.

Mental Health Foundation, *Mental Illness: The Fundamental Facts*, Mental Health Foundation, 1990.

PATMORE, C., and WEAVER, T., *Community Mental Health Teams: Lessons for Planners and Managers*, Good Practices in Mental Health, 1991.

RAFTERY, J., 'Reforming mental health services in the UK: A US Comparison', submitted for publication, 1991.

RENSHAW, J., 'Mythology and the media', *New Directions*, Good Practices in Mental Health, Spring 1990.

Research and Development for Psychiatry, *Community Mental Health Services in Britain: The Pace of Development*, Research and Development for Psychiatry, 1989.

RYAN, P., FORD, R., and CLIFFORD, P., *Case Management and Community Care*, Research and Development for Psychiatry, 1991.

SHERLOCK, J., *At Home in the Community*, Good Practices in Mental Health, 1991.

SMITH, J., and BIRCHWOOD, M., 'Relatives and patients as partners in the management of schizophrenia', *British Journal of Psychiatry*, No. 156, 1990, pp. 654–60.

Social Services Inspectorate, *Care Management and Assessment: Managers' Guide*, HMSO, 1991.

WALID, A., and McCARTHY, M., 'Community psychiatric care for homeless people in inner London', *Health Trends*, No. 21, 1989, pp. 67–9.

WELLER, B., 'Crisis at Christmas', *Lancet* (i), 1987, pp. 553–54.

WHITEHEAD, A., 'Accrediting the accreditors', *Community Care*, 10 January 1991.

Chapter 10

Department of the Environment, *The Internal Management of Local Authorities in England*, HMSO, 1991.

Department of Health, *Caring for People: Community Care in the Next Decade and Beyond*, HMSO, 1989.

Price Waterhouse, *Implementing Community Care – Purchaser, Commissioner and Provider Roles*, Department of Health/Price Waterhouse, 1991.

Chapter 11

HARDING, T., *Great Expectations*, Policy Forum Paper 1, National Institute for Social Work, London, 1992.

Chapter 12

AUSTIN, M.J., *Managing at a Time of Cuts*, Research paper presented at a seminar in Edinburgh University, 1984.

CARNALL, C.A., *Managing Change in Organisations*, Prentice Hall, London, 1990.

Department of Health, *Caring for People: Community Care in the Next Decade and Beyond*, Cmnd.849, HMSO, 1989.

GLENNERSTER, H., *Planning for Priority Groups*, Martin Robertson, Oxford, 1983.

GRIFFITHS, SIR R., *Community Care: Agenda for Action*, HMSO, 1988.

MARRIS, P., *Loss and Change*, R.K.P., London, 1986.

PARKES, C.M., *Bereavement: Studies of Grief in Adult Life*, Tavistock Publications, London, 1972.

SMILEY, C., 'Managing Agreement – the Abeline Paradox', *Community Development Journal*, Vol.17, no.1, 1982.

TOFFLER, A., *Future Shock*, Bodley Head, London, 1970.

Chapter 13

ALLSOP, J., 'Primary health care: the implications of recent changes', in ALLEN, I., ed., *Health and Social Services: the New Relationship*, Policy Studies Institute, 1991.

BEARDSHAW, V., and TOWELL, D., *Assessment and Case Management*, Briefing Paper No.10, King's Fund College, 1990.

BLAND, R., and BLAND, R.E. *Client Characteristics and Patterns of Care in Local Authority Old People's Homes*, University of Stirling mimeo, 1985.

BLAND, R.E., HUDSON, H.M. and DOBSON, B.M., *The EPIC Evaluation, Interim Report*, University of Stirling mimeo, 1992.

BOOTH, T., et al., 'Psychiatric Crises in the Community: Collaboration and the 1983 Mental Health Act', in HOROBIN, G., ed., *Responding to Mental Illness*, Research Highlights, No.11, Kogan Page, London, 1985.

BROWN, R., 'Social work in mental health teams: the local authority field social worker', in TAYLOR, R., and FORD, J., *Social Work and Health Care*, Jessica Kingsley, 1989.

CARTLIDGE, A., BOND, J., and GREGSON, B., 'Interprofessional Collaboration in Primary Health Care', *Nursing Times*, 83, 46, 1987 in DALLEY, G., 1989.

CHALLIS, D., 'Case management: problems and possibilities' in ALLEN, I., ed., *Care Managers and Care Management*, Policy Studies Institute, 1991.

CHALLIS, D., and DAVIES, B., *Case Management in Community Care*, Gower, 1986.

DALLEY, G., 'Professional ideology or organisational tribalism? The health service–social work divide' in TAYLOR, R., and FORD, J., *Social Work and Health Care*, Jessica Kingsley, 1989.

DAVIES, B., BEBBINGTON, A., CHARNELY,H., et al., *Resources, Needs and Outcomes in Community-based Care*, Avebury Gower, 1990.

Department of Health, *Community Care in the Next Decade and Beyond: Policy Guidance*, HMSO, 1990.

REFERENCES

Department of Health, *Caring for People: Community Care in the Next Decade and Beyond*, HMSO, 1989.

GOLDBERG, E.M., and CONNELLY, N., *The Effectiveness of Social Care for the Elderly*, Heinemann, 1982.

House of Commons 329, First Report from the Select Committee on Violence in the Family, Session 1976–7, Violence to Children, Vol. II Evidence, in HALLETT, C., and STEVENSON, O., *Child Abuse: Aspects of Interprofessional Co-operation*, George Allen and Unwin, 1980.

HUMPHREYS, J., BLUNDEN, R., WILSON, C., NEWMAN, T., and PAGLER, J., 'Planning for Progress, Research Report No. 18, Mental Handicap in Wales Applied Research Unit, University of Wales, Cardiff, 1985.

HUNTER, D., et al., *Patterns and Pathways in the Care of Elderly People*, Final Report to the Chief Scientist Office's Health Services Research Committee, University of Aberdeen mimeo, 1987.

HUNTINGTON, J., 'Social work and general medical practice, *Collaboration or Conflict*, Allen and Unwin, 1981.

JENKINS, J., FELCE, D., TOOGOOD, S., MANSELL, J., and DE KOCK, U., *Individual Programme Planning: A Mechanism for Development Plans to Meet the Specific Needs of Individuals with Mental Handicaps*, British Institute of Mental Handicap, 1988.

KAHN, A., 'Institutional constraints to interprofessional practice', in HALLETT, C., and STEVENSON, O., *Child Abuse: Aspects of Interprofessional Co-operation*, George Allen and Unwin, 1980.

LOWE, K., and DE PAIVA, S., *NIMROD: an Overview*, HMSO, 1991.

NEILL, J., SINCLAIR, I., GORBACH, P., and WILLIAMS, J., *A Need for Care? Elderly Applicants for Local Authority Homes*, Avebury Gower, 1988.

RENSHAW, J., HAMPSON, R., THOMASON, C., DARTON, R., JUDGE, K., and KNAPP, M., *Care in the Community: The First Steps*, Gower, 1988.

SINCLAIR, I., ed., *Residential Care: the Research Reviewed*, HMSO, 1988.

Social Services Inspectorate, *From Home Help to Home Care: an Analysis of Policy, Resourcing and Service Management*, SSI, 1987.

Social Services Inspectorate, *Assessment Systems and Community Care*, HMSO, 1991.

Social Services Inspectorate/Social Work Services Group, *Care Management and Assessment Practitioners' Guide*, HMSO, 1991.

The National Health Service and Community Care Act, 1990, HMSO

WESTLAND, P., 'The Community Health Services: a new relationship' in ALLEN, I., ed., *Health and Social Services: the New Relationship*, Policy Studies Institute, 1991.

Chapter 14

AUDIT COMMISSION, *Making a Reality of Community Care*, HMSO, 1986.

BRANDON, D., 'Seven confusions about service brokerage', *Community Living*, October 1989.

CHALLIS, D., and DAVIES, B., *Case Management and Community Care*, Gower, 1986.

182

DAVIES, K., 'Old medicine is still no community care' in *Community Care*, 27 September 1990.

Department of Health, *Caring for People: Community Care in the Next Decade and Beyond*, HMSO, 1989.

Department of Health, *Caring for People: Community Care in the Next Decade and Beyond: Practice Guidance*, HMSO, 1990.

PALMER, E., RITCHIE, P., ROWLEY, D., and TAYLOR, E., *Planning and Managing Community*, University of Dundee, 1991.

PECK, E., RITCHIE, P., and SMITH, H., *Contracting and Case Management in Community Care*, Paper 32, CCETSW, London, 1991.

Social Services Inspectorate/Social Work Services Group, *Care Management and Assessment – Practitioners' Guide and Managers' Guide*, HMSO, 1991.

WEIL, M., *Case Management in Human Service*, Jossey Bass, 1985.

Chapter 15

FORSTER, M., *Have the Men had Enough?*, Penguin, 1990.

HAFFENDEN, S., *Setting up Services for Carers – a Practitioner's Guide*, HMSO, 1990.

KOHNER, N., *Caring at Home: Handbook for Carers*, National Extension College, 1989.

PARKER, G., *With Due Care and Attention*, Family Policy Studies Centre, 1990 (2nd edition).

PITKEATHLEY, J., *It's my Duty, Isn't It?* Souvenir, 1989.

RICHARDSON, A., UNELL, J., and ASTON, B., *A New Deal for Carers*, King's Fund, 1989.

Social Services Committee of House of Commons, *Community Care: Carers*, Fifth Report, HMSO, 1990.

TWIGG, J., ATKIN, K and PERRING, C., *Carers and Services*, HMSO, 1990.

Chapter 16

ASH, A., MILNER, L., and RITCHIE, P., *Quality in Action*, Norah Fry Research Centre, Bristol, 1991.

CULLEN, HON. LORD, Public Enquiry into the Piper Alpha Disaster, HMSO, 1990.

MAXWELL, R.J., 'Quality assessment in health perspectives in NHS management', *British Medical Journal*, 288, 12 May 1984.

O'BRIEN, J., and LYLE, C., *Framework for Accomplishment*, Georgia, Responsive Systems Associates, 1988.

ROBSON, M., *Quality Circles in Action*, Gower, 1984.

SMITH, H., and MANSELL, J., *Determining Quality in Community Care Services*, forthcoming.

Social Sevices Inspectorate, *Homes are for Living In*, HMSO, 1990.

WOLFENSBERGER, W., and GLENN, L., PASS 3, National Institute of Mental Retardation, Toronto, 1975.

Chapter 17

Department of Health, *Inspecting for Quality*, HMSO, 1991.
National Health Service and Community Care Act, HMSO, 1990.
WAGNER, G., *Residential Care: A Positive Choice*, HMSO, 1988.

Index

quality management 111

rationing 21, 135, 140
residential services 9, 89, 124, 157,
    160, 163, 165, 168
respite care 146
risk management 26, 27, 32
  adult protection 29–33

service co-ordination 49–51, 63, 126,
    136
standard spending assessments
    110
stereotypes 129

substitute decision makers 28, 30

users
  choice 13, 19, 28, 79–80,
    131
  involvement 10, 26, 137, 140, 157,
    158, 160, 165–168
  satisfaction 22, 36
  voluntary sector 69

value for money 107
voluntary sector 9, 11, 64–66
  ethnic minorities 37–39
  housing 59